Hollywood
HUNKS
AND HEROES

Daniel and Susan Cohen

First Published in 1985 by

Bison Books Ltd
176 Old Brompton Road
London SW5
England

Copyright © 1985 Bison Books Ltd

ISBN 0-86124-233-5

Printed in Hong Kong

page 1: *The sexiest spy of the sixties, James Bond, as played by Sean Connery, waits for a damsel in distress, or a SMERSH agent.*

Below: *As Jett Rink in* Giant *(1956), James Dean capped his brief career of playing misunderstood loners.*

Contents

Introduction

On screen they walk tall, larger than life but no bigger than our dreams. Hollywood hunks and heroes. Masculine to the core, each stands for something and each is unique. Imitators beware: whether they're cowboys, tough guys or suave lovers, these men are the stuff of our fantasies. In a dark theater, they're film magic. They're what women want and what men want to be.

Some appeal only to one sex; some appeal only to the other. Humphrey Bogart, Hollywood's greatest legendary hero, appeals to both. Everybody's favorite cynic turned idealist, he is without equal. There'll never be another one like him again. But there'll never be another Cary Grant either. Who could ever rival his slightly embarrassed classy cool? And there will never be an heir to the throne of Hollywood's king, Clark Gable. Like Bogart's Rick, Gable's Rhett is forever.

But some of our greatest heroes are still making movies, Robert Redford and Paul Newman are good actors and certainly the best looking pair around. For vivid personalities there's Marlon Brando. From Stanley Kowalski to the Godfather, from tee shirts to tissue paper, he's charisma in the flesh. For sheer energy there's Warren Beatty, whose list of films is impressive. His list of girlfriends is even longer. Tom Selleck wows women with beefcake; Burt Reynolds does it with humor; Omar Sharif does it with an accent; and Richard Gere does it nude.

Left: *Robert Redford co-starred with Natalie Wood in* Inside Daisy Clover *(1965), the story of an adolescent movie star in Hollywood in the 1930s.*
Above: *Trying to break out of the 'Rocky' mold, Sylvester Stallone played an embittered Vietnam-War vet on the rampage in* First Blood *(1982). The critics were not impressed.*

Above: *Released after his death*, Rebel without a Cause *(1955) was responsible for James Dean's reputation as the prototype fifties rebel. The film gave Natalie Wood one of her first adult roles.*

Right: *The role of the possibly-murderous playboy-husband in* Suspicion *(1941) was a change of pace for Cary Grant, but his co-star, Joan Fontaine, was the one to capture the Oscar.*

Hunks come in different shapes and types. Sylvester Stallone is an ethnic hunk but as Rocky he's an all-American hero, too. And speaking of American heroes, John Wayne was one hundred percent red, white and blue and the number one box office draw for a generation. He's gone now but Clint Eastwood is still around to prove that toughness and masculinity are still tops at the box office.

Gary Cooper was the strong silent type who showed us it was okay for real men to have morals. Errol Flynn showed us that if you looked good in tights, morals were distinctly expendable. Sean Connery has a rugged charm that appeals to both men and women. Men thought Valentino a lounge lizard. Women considered him a panther. Richard Burton got a lot of help from Liz Taylor and William Shakespeare. And then there's Jimmy Dean, hero of the young, because he died so young, one of Hollywood's greatest stars.

We admire them, we care about them. When it comes to Hollywood hunks and heroes we can be glad it's a man's world.

Warren Beatty

Warren Beatty (that's Beetee or Baytee, it doesn't matter which; he uses either pronunciation depending on the mood he's in) is bold, powerful, ambitious, intelligent and larger than life. That makes him a hero. He's also a sexy playboy who loves to party and that makes him a hunk. Beatty's beauties include Natalie Wood, Joan Collins, Julie Christie, Liv Ullmann, etc., etc. Woody Allen, when asked what he would like to return as in another life said, "Warren Beatty's fingertips."

Warren Beatty was born in 1937 in Richmond, Virginia. Beatty's parents were teachers who cared about the arts and while their talented daughter, who would one day be famous as Shirley MacLaine, took dancing lessons, their son read books and played the piano. Beatty also played football. Turning down several athletic scholarships he went to Northwestern University to study drama, quitting at the end of his first year to go to New York. Once there, Beatty performed in summer stock and on television but he was soon spotted by playwright William Inge who cast him in *A Loss of Roses* on Broadway in 1959. A dazzling film debut followed in *Splendor in the Grass* (60), with Natalie Wood. Beatty preferred movies to theater and he gladly abandoned New York for California where from the very beginning he asked for and commanded an exceptionally high salary.

But the two movies that came after *Splendor in the Grass*, *The Roman Spring of Mrs Stone* (61) and *All Fall Down* (62), weren't commercial successes. Beatty, footloose and

bored by material possessions, didn't seem to care. Possessed of demons and visions all his own, the young Warren Beatty was energetic, hard driving, and hard to get along with. So Hollywood labeled him a rebel and a maverick and waited for him to mess up. He didn't.

Lilith (64) and *Mickey One* (65) were fine films but Beatty wanted to be more than an actor. When a script came his way about a pair of depression hoods who were also star-crossed lovers, he worked feverishly to produce it. The movie was *Bonnie and Clyde* (67). The film, an enormous success, made a star of the unknown Faye Dunaway, and legitimized a new high level of screen violence. Though now much in demand Beatty was to turn down a slew of potential hits over the next few years, including *Butch Cassidy and the Sundance Kid*, *The Way We Were* and *Last Tango in Paris* because he wanted to make his own movies his own way.

He was also involved in the heated politics of the late 1960s which took a lot of his time. Active in the campaigns of several liberal and left-leaning candidates, Beatty considered going into politics himself. He may yet do so. Films are not the only thing in his life.

Beatty made *McCabe and Mrs Miller* (71) with Julie Christie and gossip columnists predicted marriage. It didn't happen. He produced and appeared in *Shampoo* (75), which was a hit. Audiences flocked to see Beatty play a hot hairdresser in this sexy film.

Heaven Can Wait (78), a charming remake of the 40s classic, *Here Comes Mr Jordan*, showed Beatty at his most appealing. He co-wrote, co-directed, and produced the film about a dead football player who gets another shot at life. The movie was nominated for Best Picture Academy Award and Beatty was nominated as Best Director (in collaboration) and Best Actor.

Left: *Probably the most personal of all of Warren Beatty's movies to date,* Reds *(1981), co-starring Diane Keaton, was the story of American radical, John Reed. It included fascinating interviews with many of the people who had known Reed, intercut with a very moving love story.*

Above: Bonnie and Clyde *(1967) was the first movie which Beatty produced. This influential film set a new standard in violence and bloodshed and made major stars out of Beatty and his co-star, Faye Dunaway.*

Right: *Set in a mental institution,* Lilith *(1964) also starred Jean Seberg. Others featured in the cast were Kim Stanley and Peter Fonda. Beatty played a trainee therapist who falls in love with a patient (Seberg).*

But for years Warren Beatty had been obsessed with the idea of bringing the story of American radical John Reed to the screen. Reed, the author of *Ten Days that Shook The World* and the only American buried in the Kremlin wall, was Beatty's idea of a hero. Financing, producing and directing this gargantuan project took Beatty years. The movie, called *Reds* (81), co-starred Beatty's chief romantic interest of the time, Diane Keaton. The picture, right down to its cutting and editing, was definitely Beatty's baby. To insure its commercial success Beatty saw to it that *Red*'s political theme never overwhelmed the love story at the core of the movie. Still, *Reds* was not the blockbuster Beatty had hoped for. *On Golden Pond* was the commercial success of the year and *Chariots of Fire* took the Oscar for Best Picture. Beatty did, however, win the Best Director Academy Award.

What's next for Warren Beatty? The late bizarre billionaire Howard Hughes may be on the agenda. If so,

Above: *James Mason (left) was among Beatty's co-stars in* Heaven Can Wait. *This 1978 remake of Ernest Lubitsch's very successful comedy,* Here Comes Mr Jordan *(1941) was written, directed and produced by Beatty.*

Left: *As the sexy hairdresser in* Shampoo *(1975), Beatty had the opportunity to seduce Julie Christie, Lee Grant, Goldie Hawn and Carrie Fisher. The script which was co-written by Beatty was nominated for an Academy Award.*

Beatty will go about the job of making a movie based on Hughes's life with the dogged determination he brings to every project.

Nobody personifies the changes in Hollywood over the past 20 years better than Beatty. As interested in camera technique and finance as in acting, he's the kind of all-round renaissance type you didn't find in Tinseltown in the days of the old studio system. Warren Beatty just may be the most complex and innovative sex symbol in movie-land's pantheon of stars. What would Louis B Mayer say about that?

Warren Beatty: *Splendor in the Grass* 60, *The Roman Spring of Mrs Stone* 61, *All Fall Down* 62, *Lilith* 64, *Mickey One* 65, *Promise Her Anything* 66, *Kaleidoscope* 66, *Bonnie and Clyde* 67, *The Only Game in Town* 69, *McCabe and Mrs Miller* 71, *$ (Dollars)* 72, *The Parallax View* 74, *Shampoo* 75, *The Fortune* 75, *Heaven Can Wait* 78, *Reds* 81.

Humphrey Bogart

Born in 1899 or thereabouts (there is some question about the date) he was named, improbably, Humphrey DeForest Bogart. It's a name P G Wodehouse might have made up. He would grow up to become America's favorite cynic, the tough guy with a heart of gold, down to earth, democratic, a no-frills type who never had the odds in his favor.

Yet Bogie (a nickname he picked up after he went into films) was no slum kid. He was born into a posh and cushy world, though the family money would disappear after he grew up and leave him a hungry young actor struggling to survive. His father was Dr Belmont DeForest Bogart. His mother, Maud Humphrey, was a famous artist and illustrator. Little Humphrey was sent to Trinity School in upper Manhattan and because his father dreamed of sending his only son to Yale, he then went to Phillips Academy in Andover, Massachusetts. His father's dream was off the mark. Bogart was no student and never made it through prep school.

Instead of college he joined the Navy but the year was 1918 and World War I ended before Bogart saw combat. Because of an accident in the Navy he acquired a scar on his lip which may have been the cause of his distinctive raspy lisp. But his lips were prominent even when he was a baby and, knowing Bogart, the lisp may just have been a matter of original style.

When Bogart got out of the Navy he had no idea what he wanted to do with his life. He needed a job and having several friends in the theater he stumbled into the position of company manager for a play called *The Ruined Lady*

which was going on tour. One thing led to another and soon he was performing on stage, though not very well. Bogart had to work hard to learn his craft. As he improved so did the reviews.

Bogart became one of Broadway's reliable romantic juveniles, appearing in a series of farces, romps and comedies with names like *Hell's Bells*, *Cradle Snatchers* and *Baby Mine*. It's hard to imagine Bogart cavorting in such roles, but he must have had something because he caught the eye of a successful actress some years his senior, Helen Menken. She was the pursuer, persuading Bogart to marry her in 1926. The marriage was brief. In 1928 Bogart got the chance to be in Maxwell Anderson's *Saturday's Children*. It was a good show and he was good in it. That same year he married again, much more willingly. Her name was Mary Phillips and she was also in the theater. This marriage lasted nine years and ended only after the couple's careers diverged. He chose Hollywood and movies; she wanted New York and the Broadway stage.

In 1930 Hollywood was in a deep crisis. Silent pictures were going the way of the dodo and movie studios were engaged in a desperate search for actors with decent voices. Bogart went west. Starting with a short film, *Broadway's Like That* (30), he knocked around Hollywood, appearing unmemorably in *A Devil With Women* (30), *Up The River* (30) starring Spencer Tracy, a war movie called *Body and Soul* (31), *Love Affair* (32) and *Big City Blues* (32). On film, as on stage, he was not an overnight sensation but he gained a good reputation for his solid working habits. Bogart showed up on the set on time, memorized his lines every night, and concentrated hard on picking up technique as he went along. This disciplined approach to the acting profession stayed with him for the rest of his life.

Left: *As the hard-drinking skipper of the* African Queen, *Humphrey Bogart played one of his most famous roles, which earned him the Academy Award for Best Actor in 1951.*

Above: *As Duke Mantee in* The Petrified Forest *(1936), with Leslie Howard and Bette Davis, Bogart had his first real film success. He had played the same part on Broadway. (The actor in the foreground is Dick Foran, who later starred in* A Connecticut Yankee *on Broadway.)*

Right: *As the cynical idealist, Rick Blaine, owner of Rick's Café Americaine in* Casablanca *(1942), Bogart played opposite Ingrid Bergman. The movie is still one of the most popular ever made and many of its lines ('Play it, Sam') are equally immortal.*

Bogart wasn't getting anywhere in movies so he returned to seek success on Broadway. But it was his wife Mary who found steady stage work keeping Bogart afloat during the first few years of the depression. Bogart's career troubles came from the simple fact that he was getting too old to play pretty boys. Yet, he was hopelessly typecast and not for the last time.

Luck plays a part in any actor's life, even one as determined as Bogart, and in 1934 he got a real break. Out of the blue he was cast as Duke Mantee, an escaped killer, in Robert E Sherwood's *The Petrified Forest*. Bogart was magnificent as the personification of menace and danger. He was a hit and so was the play.

The star of the play was Leslie Howard and when Warner Brothers bought the script, Howard promised Bogart that he would fight to have him play Duke in the movie. Warner's had Edward G Robinson under contract and they could care less about this unknown, Bogart. But Howard was true to his word. *The Petrified Forest* (36) included Bogart and a very young Bette Davis in the cast. The movie was popular and it decided Bogart's future. He would stick with Hollywood films and bid the Broadway stage farewell.

There was no hint of the romantic juvenile in Bogart's new incarnation. But there was no hint of the hero he was to become either. Ranked below James Cagney, George Raft and Edward G Robinson as a movie tough guy and gangster, Bogart was a vicious meanie in film after film. Since the movie-going audiences of the time believed bad guys should always get their comeuppence, Bogart usually died on screen in a variety of gruesome ways such as electrocution or hanging. Once in a while he lucked out and was sent to jail for life. His name was generally below the title when they ran movie credits, a sign of his plebian status. Bogart kept trying to break out of the gangster image but he believed in taking any work that came his way and he had no use for petulance and temperament. So he kept on shooting and dying on film.

In *Bullets or Ballots* (36), he played a cop squaring off against Edward G Robinson. In *Isle of Fury* (36) he looked silly in a pencil-line moustache. Bogart was a crook in *The Great O'Malley* (37) and another crook in *San Quentin* (37). He gave an excellent performance as a DA in *Marked Woman* (37), and a boxing promoter in *Kid Galahad* (37), the two really important films of the period. He did *Stand-In* (37) with Leslie Howard. *Swing Your Lady* (38) was a

Above: *Mary Astor enlists the aid of Jerome Cowan and Bogart of the detective firm Spade and Archer in* The Maltese Falcon *(1941)*.

Above: *The prospectors searching for* The Treasure of the Sierra Madre *(1948) were (left to right) Bruce Bennett, Tim Holt, Bogart, and Walter Huston, who won an Academy Award as Best Supporting Actor.*
Below: *To Have and Have Not (1944) co-starred Bogart with newcomer Lauren Bacall. They were married the following year, and made three more movies,* The Big Sleep, Dark Passage *and* Key Largo.

hillbilly farce so embarrassing it gave Bogart the shudders.

In 1938 Bogart married Mayo Methot, an attractive blond who had a small part in *Marked Woman*. Thus began the saga of the battling Bogarts. It was a turbulent relationship leaving behind a trail of broken crockery, drunken scenes and violent encounters. The pair spent a lot of time on their boat, aptly named *Sluggy*. However, Mayo did share Bogart's lifelong love of dogs and she was devoted to his career, supporting his attempts to play something more stirring and romantic than a demented murderer.

Unfortunately, *The Amazing Dr Clitterhouse* (38) had Bogart as a gun-wielding heavy once more. He was a crooked lawyer in the outstanding *Angels With Dirty Faces* (38), opposite Cagney. The long suffering Bogart found himself the *King of the Underworld* (39), and a bootlegger in *The Roaring Twenties* (39). *Dark Victory* (39) was a fine film offering Bogart a change of pace as Bette Davis's Irish groom, but he was doomed to playing a mobster again in *Invisible Stripes* (39). He was a nasty double crosser and gangster boss in *Brother Orchid* (40), and with Raft in *They Drive By Night* (40), Bogart was a tough truck driver.

Had Bogart's movie career ended at this point he would have gone down in the annals of Hollywood as a solid film thug, a hard-working, reasonable, no-nonsense sort of actor, a real pro. Then opportunity presented itself again.

High Sierra (41) had been rejected by several major Hollywood stars. Bogart's habit of never quibbling over a part stood him in good stead and he said yes to the film. He played a gangster as usual but a gangster with a tender side and a streak of humanity. When he died at the end of the picture the audience felt sorry for him. *High Sierra* started Bogart on his route to becoming a hero. The movie's success insured that from now on he would receive top billing. It also brought him the role of Sam Spade in *The Maltese Falcon* (41), certainly one of the best movies ever to come out of Hollywood. Bogart was offered the film only after other more famous actors turned it down. They didn't want to take a chance on a brand new director, former script writer John Huston. Bogart took that chance. It was the smartest thing he ever did.

Bogart believed that a professional owes it to his audience to give them the best performance he's capable of, whether the material he has to work with is good or bad. In this case the material was terrific, making it easier for Bogart to give *The Maltese Falcon* his all. Based on the Dashiell Hammett mystery the movie script wove a tale of greed, violence and the pursuit of the stuff that dreams are made of. The movie was perfectly cast, with Mary Astor, Sydney Greenstreet, Peter Lorre and Elisha Cook Jr acting as ideal foils for Bogart. It's one of Hollywood's immortal movies and generations of fans have memorized the film scene by scene. Bogart emerges at last in his final persona, a smart tough guy, dangerous when cornered or challenged, who's capable of showing integrity when it really counts. He was proud of the film.

The coming of the Second World War made Americans hungry for screen heroes and who was better than Bogart to battle a Nazi spy ring in *All Through The Night* (42). *Across The Pacific* (42) was a Maltese Falcon reunion bringing together John Huston, Mary Astor, Sydney Greenstreet and Bogart. This time the Japanese were the villains. But *Casablanca* (42) dwarfed these efforts. It is Bogart's most famous film, arguably the best movie Hollywood ever made, and a cult classic since the 1960s. *Casablanca* won the Academy Award for Best Picture, brought Bogart his first Best Actor nomination, made a fortune and established Bogart as the 1940s equivalent of a superstar. A new contract, negotiated at the time, had him playing the character of Rick Blaine to the tune of a $3500 a week salary.

The movie is set in early 1941 before Pearl Harbor. Casablanca seethes with refugees trying to escape the Nazis. Rick is a nightclub owner who fought on the Loyalist side in Spain who wants to stay uninvolved and uncommitted. Brooding over a lost love and otherwise minding his own business, Rick's life is transformed when the very woman he loves and never expected to see again walks into his nightclub. Her name is Ilsa Lund and she is beautifully played by the beautiful Ingrid Bergman. After a number of stirring scenes which could never be improved upon, the movie winds up with Rick valiantly renouncing Ilsa because she is needed by her husband, virtuous resistance leader Victor Laszlo, played by Paul Henreid. Then Rick, accompanied by Casablanca's cynical police chief (a role immortalized by Claude Rains), goes off to fight the Nazis himself. He has made his commitment and comes alive in the process. The deeply moved, frequently weeping audiences who saw *Casablanca* assumed the picture was under tight control from the start, it flowed so smoothly and flawlessly. Actually *Casablanca* was an incredible mishmash. The set was in chaos from day one of shooting. The script was a mess. Nobody knew for sure how the picture would end, leaving Bogart and Bergman half-crazed wrecks, actors trying to do their best under, to say the least, trying conditions. The result was a masterpiece.

Bogart's position in movies was now totally secure. From 1943 to 1949 he was on the top ten Hollywood star list, and one of Warner Brothers' major performers. *Action in the North Atlantic* (43) was an elaborate picture, featuring explosive special effects. *Passage to Marseilles* (44) was another war movie. But the only other stand-out film of the era besides *Casablanca* Bogart made was *To Have and Have Not* (44), more or less based on the Ernest Hemingway novel and directed by Howard Hawks. Bogart played opposite a 20-year-old ex-model named Lauren Bacall, who was to become a legend in her own right later. It didn't take Bogart long to discover that Bacall was the love of his life and the screen sizzled accordingly. In this movie Bacall uttered her famous line, 'If you want me, just whistle,' and proceeded to give the kiss of death to Bogart's stormy marriage to Mayo.

Bogie and Baby, as the columnists like to refer to them, were married on 21 May 1945. It was one of the most successful Hollywood marriages ever, lasting the rest of Bogart's life. Two children were born to the Bogarts, a son named Steve and a daughter called Leslie Howard.

On screen the couple worked together in *The Big Sleep* (46), a *film noir* based on a Raymond Chandler private eye novel. The movie's plot was and remains totally incomprehensible but Bogart and Bacall gave the picture style. Warners rewarded Bogart with a generous contract granting him enormous freedom and money, $200,000 per film plus $1000 a week expenses for location work.

1947 was the year the Cold War began to descend on Hollywood and the House Committee on Un-American Activities took a look at the motion picture industry. John Huston organized a group of stars and other Hollywood professionals to fly to Washington and attend a hearing in support of writers, directors and producers who had been called to testify before the committee but who had refused to co-operate. The Bogarts went along, which got a lot of press attention. Bogart had nothing to do with any further political activities. To some this was cowardice, to others merely a reflection of his general lack of interest in public issues. In 1952 he supported Adlai Stevenson when he ran for the Presidency. Otherwise, Bogart's life was essentially a private one. He was devoted to his wife and family, chess, and his beautiful sail boat, *Santana*. His other big interest was work, making movies.

1947 was also the year Bogart set up his own movie company, Santana Pictures Corporation. He was the first actor of the postwar era to do this, though many would follow, and Warner Brothers didn't like the idea at all. Bogart fought it out with them and won, releasing the first Santana film, *Dead Reckoning* (47) with Lizabeth Scott through Columbia. For Warner's he did *The Treasure of the Sierra Madre* (48), a magnificent movie about gold fever filmed in Mexico. Bogart was brilliant as an ordinary man dehumanized by greed. But the film belonged to Walter Huston, who won the Academy Award for Best Supporting Actor for his masterful performance. His son John won for Best Director and Best Screenplay. Bogart wasn't even nominated.

Key Largo (48) had Bogart and Bacall back together on screen again. *Knock on Any Door* (49) was a Santana film based on the popular Willard Motley novel. Like other Santana films it was well meaning. Bogart formed his own company partly because he wanted the freedom to make good movies. However, to date nothing from Santana had matched his achievements at Warner's. He was a pilot in *Chain Lightning* (50) at Warner's and a screenwriter in *A Lonely Place* (50) at Santana. His last movie at Warner's was *The Enforcer* (51). After that Bogart worked with independent producers, various studios, whatever appealed to him that he could get or put together himself.

Once again Bogart was to owe something to the genius of John Huston, this time for *The African Queen* (51) with Katharine Hepburn. Based on the C S Forester novel about an old drunk and old maid who fall in love on an old boat, *The African Queen* ranks with Bogart's greatest films. Despite the hardships of filming on location in Africa, the movie's charm, spirit and superb acting reflect a sure and easy touch. It was an unlikely love story to appeal to a public geared to romance for the young and beautiful but it was a big hit. At last Bogart got his much deserved Academy Award, all the sweeter because those in the know were sure it would go to Marlon Brando for his role as Stanley Kowalski in *A Streetcar Named Desire*.

Beat the Devil (54) was a delightful crime spoof, written by Truman Capote. It became an instant cult film. *The Caine Mutiny* (54) had Bogart cast as a frightening but sympathetic Captain Queeg. He was in *Sabrina* with Audrey Hepburn in 1954, a year that also saw him playing opposite Ava Gardner in *The Barefoot Contessa* (54). Both movies were changes of pace for Bogart. Among the best of his later movies was *We're No Angels* (55), a charming little film which allowed Bogart to be a lovable convict and a do-gooder besides. *The Desperate Hours* (55) let Bogart revert to type. He played a brutal murderer once again. His last picture was *The Harder They Fall* (56). He played a battered and seedy journalist who turns honest and admirable at the end. He was hard at work when he found out he had cancer in 1956. He endured painful surgery but died on 13 January 1957.

He wasn't a mirror image of the heroic character he created on film, no man is. He had his detractors, people who found him insufferably rude or felt he drank far too much. But he had plenty of supporters as well, people who admired his charm and kindness. He hated phonies and pretense, followed his own code and behaved professionally and personally with honor. That makes him a lot like Sam Spade and Rick after all. He made some of the best films Hollywood ever produced, is revered as an actor by every new generation to come along and is perhaps the premier male movie star of all times.

Quite an achievement! Here's looking at you, kid.

Humphrey Bogart: *Broadway's Like That* 30, *A Devil With Women* 30, *Up The River* 30, *Body and Soul* 31, *Bad Sister* 31, *Women of All Nations* 31, *A Holy Terror* 31, *Love Affair* 32, *Big City Blues* 32, *Three on a Match* 32, *Midnight* 34, *The Petrified Forest* 36, *Bullets or Ballots* 36, *Two Against the World* 36, *China Clipper* 36, *Isle of Fury* 36, *Black Legion* 37, *The Great O'Malley* 37, *Marked Woman* 37, *Kid Galahad* 37, *San Quentin* 37, *Dead End* 37, *Stand-In* 37, *Swing Your Lady* 38, *Crime School* 38, *Men Are Such Fools* 38, *The Amazing Dr Clitterhouse* 38, *Racket Busters* 38, *Angels With Dirty Faces* 38, *King of the Underworld* 39, *The Oklahoma Kid* 39, *Dark Victory* 39, *You Can't Get Away With Murder* 39, *The Roaring Twenties* 39, *The Return of Dr X* 39, *Invisible Stripes* 39, *Virginia City* 40, *It All Came True* 40, *Brother Orchid* 40, *They Drive By Night* 40, *High Sierra* 41, *The Wagons Roll At Night* 41, *The Maltese Falcon* 41, *All Through The Night* 42, *The Big Shot* 42, *Across The Pacific* 42, *Casablanca* 42, *Action in the North Atlantic* 43, *Thank Your Lucky Stars* 43, *Sahara* 43, *Passage to Marseilles* 44, *Report From the Front* 44, *To Have and Have Not* 44, *Conflict* 45, *Hollywood Victory Caravan* 45, *Two Guys From Milwaukee* 46, *The Big Sleep* 46, *Dead Reckoning* 47, *The Two Mrs Carrolls* 47, *Dark Passage* 47, *Always Together* 48, *The Treasure of Sierra Madre* 48, *Key Largo* 48, *Knock on Any Door* 49, *Tokyo Joe* 49, *Chain Lightning* 50, *In A Lonely Place* 50, *Deadline-USA* 50, *The Enforcer* 51, *The African Queen* 51, *US Savings Bond Short* 52, *Battle Circus* 53, *Beat The Devil* 54, *The Caine Mutiny* 54, *Sabrina* 54, *We're No Angels* 55, *The Left Hand of God* 55, *The Desperate Hours* 55, *The Harder They Fall* 56.

Claude Rains orders a round-up of the usual suspects, as Paul Henried, Bogart, and Ingrid Bergman look on, at the end of Casablanca.

Marlon Brando

F or raw talent nobody beats Marlon Brando. He's a master mimic with strong powers of observation, a genius at finding the right gesture to convey the things that can't be expressed in words. He is innovative, spontaneous and a born scene stealer whose presence fills even the widest of wide screens. He's a presence off screen as well. Loved and hated, admired and scorned, Marlon Brando is always controversial.

He was born in Omaha, Nebraska, in 1924. His mother was a talented amateur actress, his father sold cattle feed. Later the family moved to Illinois where Marlon, nicknamed 'Bud', grew up playing football and drums. But Brando was never the model Midwestern All-American kid. He was so rebellious and undisciplined that his worried father sent him to military school hoping he'd shape up. Brando didn't. Expelled from military school, he promptly took off for New York to become an actor.

Many actors have had to struggle to survive. Not Brando. Strong, good-looking and incredibly gifted, he quickly became respected actress Stella Adler's prize pupil. Later he was the star of the class at the Actors' Studio, where the Stanislavsky method was taught. In essence, 'The Method', as it was called, stressed self-absorption and introspection as the means of finding one's way to an interpretation of character. Brando would be the first American 'Method' actor to make it big in films.

In 1944 Brando made his Broadway debut playing Nels in John Van Druten's *I Remember Mama*. The play was a

hit. Its homespun values appealed to a homefront audience at a time when World War II still raged. Brando was never in the service. He was 4F, due to a knee injury he received playing football back in high school. Two years later Brando appeared in *Truckline Café*, and the critics voted him 'Broadway's Most Promising Actor.' He played Marchbanks in George Bernard Shaw's *Candida*, starring Katherine Cornell, and he toured in *The Eagle Has Two Heads* with Tallulah Bankhead. Then came the role which would catapault him into stardom. He was picked to play Stanley Kowalski in Tennessee Williams's *A Streetcar Named Desire*.

Brando's performance was a *tour de force*. He detested the brutal Stanley but he was fascinated by him and he was never satisfied with his portrayal. Night after night Brando kept recreating and changing his role so that the other actors on stage with him never knew quite what to expect. Even so, Brando found the long run of *Streetcar* almost interminable. He got bored doing the same thing day after day.

Though Brando disdained Hollywood he accepted Stanley Kramer's offer to play a paraplegic veteran in *The Men* (50) for a whopping $50,000 fee. Brando moved into a veteran's hospital, observing the injured men around him and literally living like one. Then he went on to give a smash performance, receiving great reviews. Despite his criticisms of Hollywood, Brando found movie acting difficult. Filming scenes out of sequence was a strain and the camera's narrow range imposed technical limits on what he could do. But at least he was free of repeating the same lines for months on end.

Elia Kazan directed the movie version of *A Streetcar Named Desire* (51), with basically the same cast that appeared on Broadway. The big change was Vivien Leigh,

Left: *As the aging Mafioso, Don Vito Corleone, in Francis Ford Coppola's blockbuster,* The Godfather *(1972), Brando gave an Academy Award-winning performance. With little obvious change, except for stuffing in his cheeks, he appeared to be an elderly Italian immigrant, who built a criminal empire, while still remaining a loving family man who delighted in playing with his grandchildren.*

Left: *In* A Streetcar Named Desire *with Vivien Leigh, Brando gave an electrifying performance as Stanley Kowalski.*
Top: *Perhaps miscast as Sky Masterson in the adaptation of Frank Loesser's* Guys and Dolls *(1955), Brando sang 'Luck Be A Lady' with Frank Sinatra.*
Right: *In the romantic drama,* Desirée, *Brando played Napoleon Bonaparte.*

who was given the part of Blanche in place of Jessica Tandy. The movie was a commercial as well as an artistic success. Vivien Leigh, Karl Malden and Kim Hunter won Academy Awards for their performances but Brando, though nominated for Best Actor lost out to Humphrey Bogart in *The African Queen*.

Viva Zapata (52), followed. Brando played the Mexican revolutionary hero so powerfully the critics couldn't rave enough, though some complained that there was a little too much Kowalski in Zapata. Even his most loyal fans confused Brando with Stanley, though the actor was clearly not a mumbling slob in a tee-shirt. Gossip columnists loved to write nasty things about the iconoclastic Brando and they gleefully spread all kinds of stories about him, true or otherwise. Brando showed them all when he decided to accept the role of Mark Antony in Shakespeare's *Julius Caesar* (53), with veteran performers James Mason and John Gielgud. Brando was splendid in the part. Both producer John Houseman and Gielgud sang his praises. For his performance Brando won another Academy Award nomination and an invitation from Gielgud to

24

appear in repertory with him in England. Brando turned the offer down.

The Wild One (54), had Brando as the rebel leader of a motorcycle gang. Brando, ever on the side of the underdog, had hoped the movie would make a strong political statement about alienated youth but the cold war was on and the cautious Hollywood censors said no. The script was changed. The intolerance of the town was played down and the film focused instead on the violence of the gang. It was banned in England until 1968. In *On The Waterfront* (54) Brando was a longshoreman and ex-boxer fighting against a corrupt union. Brando's sensitive performance won him an Academy Award at last, as well as The New York Critics' Best Actor Award, the Best Foreign Actor Award in Britain and the Picturegoer Gold Medal. The film itself won an Academy Award for Best Picture. Brando's career was at its peak. He was young, rich, and at the top.

He decided to show the world how versatile he could be. He played Napoleon in *Desiree* (54), a costume romance. He did a musical, *Guys and Dolls* (55), a comedy,

The Teahouse of the August Moon (56), and *Sayonara* (57), in which he played a bigoted American Air Force officer in love with a Japanese woman. In *The Young Lions* (58) Brando developed an unusual character, a Nazi officer with a conscience. He was criticized for this but Brando was never the kind of actor to play it safe. Brando was now among the top ten box-office stars. The wheel of fortune was about to take a downward spin.

First of all there was his private life. In 1957 he married Anna Kashfi, presumably an Indian woman from Calcutta. It turned out she was Joanna O'Callaghan from Wales. The marriage didn't last long but the couple had a son and for years there were stormy custody battles in the courts. It wasn't the last marriage for Brando and more well-publicized high jinks were to follow.

His next three pictures, *The Fugitive Kind* (60), *One-Eyed Jacks* (61), and *Mutiny on the Bounty* (62), lost scads of money. *One-Eyed Jacks*, a western, was the first production undertaken by Brando's own company, called Pennebaker, his mother's maiden name. Originally to be directed by Stanley Kubrick, it wound up directed by Brando instead, who spent a lot of money and alienated a lot of people. *Mutiny on the Bounty* cast Brando as a foppish Fletcher Christian and Trevor Howard as Captain Bligh. The movie was awash in expense and troubles from the start, but because of the film Brando discovered Tahiti, his favorite spot on earth.

Brando was good in *The Ugly American* (63), and in *Reflections in a Golden Eye* (67), directed by John Huston. Really, he was good in everything he did during the 60s but the movies chosen were rarely worthy of his talents. As a result his popularity declined and detractors wrote him off as another great theater actor who sold out.

The Godfather (72) did a lot to restore Brando's reputation. He played Don Vito Corleone to perfection and the tissue he stuffed in his mouth to enhance his jowls became almost as famous as the torn tee-shirt of Stanley Kowalski. Director Francis Ford Coppola had to fight the Paramount bigwigs to get Brando. They considered him wasteful and slothful. But Coppola was right, since in the end Brando was a major reason why *The Godfather* was one of the stunning successes of all time.

Now Brando, the risk taker, appeared in an X-rated film, *Last Tango in Paris* (72). Brando was allowed to 'be Brando,' creating portions of the dialogue himself based on his own life experiences. The movie caused a furor. So did Brando's refusal of the Academy Award he won for *The Godfather*. Brando had been a strong supporter of liberal causes for years, including the Civil Rights movement of the 1960s. He often chose to appear in movies with a social theme, even though the films did not always succeed on those terms.

Brando's deepest commitment was to American Indians. He sent Sacheen Littlefeather in full Apache dress to the Academy Award ceremonies in his stead to reject the award and read a statement he'd written on the plight of the Indians. As might be expected this created quite a stir.

The Missouri Breaks (76) co-starred Jack Nicholson. Brando made millions for a brief stint in *Superman* (78). He presented an unusual interpretation of a jungle comman-

Above: *The confrontation with his brother Charlie (Rod Steiger) in* On the Waterfront *(1954) was another memorable Brando performance.*
Left: *A Countess from Hong Kong (1967) co-starred Brando with Sophia Loren. The film was directed by Charlie Chaplin.*
Right: *The role of the mysterious Captain Kurtz in* Apocalypse Now *(1979) marks Brando's latest appearance on screen.*

der in Coppola's anti-Vietnam War film, *Apocalypse Now* (79), proving he could still mystify and astonish on screen.

To this day Marlon Brando is an enigma. Is he a lazy actor, contemptuous of the public, who uses cue cards during filming because he can't be bothered learning his lines? Or is he simply at his most creative improvising dialogue? Is he a vivid potent force on camera or a ham chewing up the celluloid? One thing is certain. If he were not a dazzling and original performer, people would have stopped asking these questions years ago.

Marlon Brando: *The Men* 50, *A Streetcar Named Desire* 51, *Viva Zapata* 52, *Julius Caesar* 53, *The Wild One* 54, *On the Waterfront* 54, *Desirée* 54, *Guys and Dolls* 55, *The Teahouse of the August Moon* 56, *Sayonara* 57, *The Young Lions* 58, *The Fugitive Kind* 60, *One-Eyed Jacks* 61, *Mutiny on the Bounty* 62, *The Ugly American* 63, *Bedtime Story* 64, *The Saboteur: Code Name Morituri* 65, *The Chase* 66, *The Appaloosa* 66, *A Countess from Hong Kong* 67, *Reflections in a Golden Eye* 67, *The Night of the Following Day* 68, *Candy* 68, *Burn* 70, *The Nightcomers* 72, *The Godfather* 72, *Last Tango in Paris* 73, *The Missouri Breaks* 76, *Superman* 78, *Apocalypse Now* 79.

Richard Burton

The beauty of his youth was gone but his face was still interesting. Richard Burton looked like an aging lion. He had wit, enormous charm, a wonderful voice and extraordinary stage presence. Great things were expected of him once. He was to be a fine Shakespearian actor, the successor to Laurence Olivier and John Gielgud. It didn't happen. Instead he married Elizabeth Taylor, a rich and famous movie star, and became himself a rich and famous movie star. One can't help but wonder if he ever regretted the choice.

He was born Richard Walter Jenkins Jr in Pontrhydfen, Wales, on 10 November 1925, twelfth in a line of 13 children. His father was a coal miner and the odds were that Richard would become a miner himself. But a teacher named Philip Burton recognized the boy's talents, made him his ward, and devoted himself to furthering Richard's acting career. Richard Jenkins became Richard Burton and went to Oxford on a scholarship.

Burton made his stage debut in *Druid's Rest* in 1943. After serving as a navigator with the Royal Air Force from 1944 to 1947 he returned to the stage in 1948. His first movie was *The Last Days of Dolwyn* (49). On the movie set he met a young Welsh actress, Sybil Williams, and married her. In 1949 Burton did *The Lady's Not For Burning* on stage in London. The play was taken to Broadway in 1950, and Burton received critical acclaim. At just 24 the poor boy from a working-class family in Wales was a successful actor. In 1951 at Stratford his interpretation of Prince Hal showed originality and greatness was predicted for him. Could Cinderella ask for anything more.

Burton made his first American movie, *My Cousin Rachel* (52), with Olivia de Havilland, then played Hamlet with the Old Vic Company at the Edinburgh Festival. He stayed with the company awhile, which gave rise to the rumor that Richard Burton would never abandon Britain and its splendid theatrical tradition for Hollywood and B pictures. *The Robe* (53) must have given his defenders pause.

Burton was one of a new breed of British actors who refused to hide their working-class origins. Burton reveled in a very un-middle class macho male image, drinking hard and chasing women. And he lived in mortal terror of ever being poor again. He was more like a boxer than an actor and perhaps this accounts for his schizoid career. On stage Burton was brilliant and expansive, and he had a good eye for picking roles. On screen he was either wooden or overblown and he showed little judgement when it came to choosing films. Only *Look Back in Anger* (58) was worthy of him.

Burton was a crowd pleaser as King Arthur in the 1961 Broadway musical *Camelot*, but he would enter his own personal Camelot when he began filming the Hollywood spectacle, *Cleopatra* (63). Elizabeth Taylor was at the peak of her fame and beauty when Burton arrived in Rome to become Mark Antony to her Cleopatra. Burton and Taylor fell in love. The 'scandale', as their affair was called, was carried on with much publicity. *Cleopatra*, which had already cost a fortune to make, was to cost even more as filming went on and on and on.

Despite all the hanky-panky *Cleopatra* did not make money, only slipping into the black years later when it was sold to television. Taylor divorced husband of the moment Eddie Fisher and Burton divorced Sybil. Then Burton married Taylor and moved into the world of yachts,

---

Left: *As the defrocked clergyman in* The Night of the Iguana *(1964) Burton co-starred with Ava Gardner, Deborah Kerr and Sue Lyon. But his real leading lady at this time was Elizabeth Taylor, whom he had met during the filming of* Cleopatra.

jewels, fat fees and fat living. Traveling with an entourage, Taylor and Burton acted like royalty and were treated as such.

The pair made movies together. *The VIPs* (62), spelled big box office, but *Becket* (64), without Liz and with Peter O'Toole, did Burton more good. He was on Broadway in *Hamlet* and Elizabeth was in the audience every night. He made one of his best movies, *The Spy Who Came in From the Cold* (65) and he and Taylor were excellent in *Who's Afraid of Virginia Woolf?* (66), based on the Edward Albee play and directed by Mike Nichols. *The Taming of the Shrew* (67) teamed Burton and Taylor again in an earthy version of Shakespeare's comedy about the war between the sexes.

After this there was trouble in paradise. Burton and Taylor (their fans preferred Liz and Dick) quarrelled publicly, separated, then went back together again. They were becoming a losing team at the box office as well. *Boom* (68) lost a bundle and in 1970 *Time* magazine called them famous bores.

It was low tide for Burton. He made a string of flops and the critics damned him with gusto. Still, Burton was able to command top dollar. Besides, if he was more boxer than actor he proved it by getting up off the mat and making *Anne of the Thousand Days* (69), a success which brought him his sixth Oscar nomination.

The Burtons divorced in the early 1970s, remarried in 1975 and redivorced in 1976. Burton later married Susan Hunt, a model who was once married to British race car driver, James Hunt. Burton threatened to retire but continued working as an actor, playing Winston Churchill on television and appearing on Broadway in *Equus* which got him a Tony Award. The film version of *Equus* (77) won him yet another Academy Award nomination.

Below: *Two legendary romances begin as the Roman general Marc Anthony (Richard Burton) meets the beautiful Queen of Egypt, Cleopatra (Elizabeth Taylor) in the 1963 blockbuster which turned their love affair into front page news.*

His career on the upswing, Burton chose to make *The Exorcist II/The Heretic* (77), a breathtakingly ghastly disaster. Why he appeared in this, one of the worst movies ever made, nobody knows. Certainly he didn't need the money.

His career on the wane, Richard Burton talked about returning to the theater as *King Lear* or of writing a novel. He did neither. He made action pictures like *The Medusa Touch* (78) and *The Wild Geese* (78). In 1983 he co-starred with ex-wife Taylor in *Private Lives* on stage. Their celebrity status pulled in the crowds, making some people wonder if Richard Burton wasn't just Mr Elizabeth Taylor after all.

Burton's sudden death in 1984 came as a shock, he was only 58 and despite his drinking appeared to have been in good health. The outpouring of grief from a public that had already seemed to have written him off as a hasbeen was surprising. Was it grief for what he had been, or what he might have been?

Richard Burton: *The Last Days of Dolwyn* 49, *Now Barrabas Was a Robber* 49, *Waterfront* 50, *The Woman With No Name* 50, *Green Grow the Rushes* 51, *My Cousin Rachel* 52, *The Desert Rats* 53, *The Robe* 53, *Prince of Players* 55, *The Rains of Ranchipur* 55, *Alexander The Great* 56, *Seawife* 57, *Bitter Victory* 57, *Look Back in Anger* 58, *The Bramble Bush* 59, *Ice Palace* 60, *The Longest Day* 62, *Cleopatra* 63, *The VIPs* 63, *Becket* 64, *The Night of the Iguana* 64, *Hamlet* 64, *What's New, Pussycat* 65, *The Sandpiper* 65, *The Spy Who Came in from the Cold* 65, *Who's Afraid of Virginia Woolf?* 66, *The Taming of the Shrew* 67, *Dr Faustus* 67, *The Comedians* 67, *Boom* 68, *Candy* 68, *Where Eagles Dare* 69, *Staircase* 69, *Anne of the Thousand Days* 69, *Raid on Rommel* 71, *Villain* 71, *Hammersmith is Out* 72, *Sutjeska* 72, *Bluebeard* 72, *The Assassination of Trotsky* 72, *Massacre in Rome* 73, *Under Milk Wood* 73, *The Voyage* 74, *The Klansman* 74, *Equus* 77, *The Exorcist II/The Heretic* 77, *The Medusa Touch* 78, *The Wild Geese* 78, *Sergeant Steiner* 79, *Absolution* 81, *Lovespell* 81, *1984* 84.

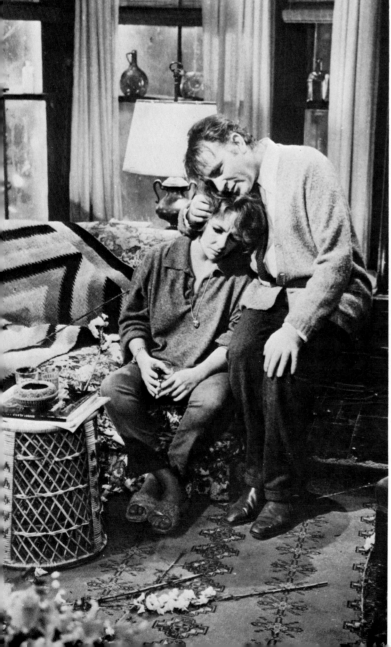

The changing face of beauty – counter clock-wise from top right:
With Jean Simmons in The Robe *(1953), Burton played an early Christian martyr.*
The Rains of Ranchipur (1955) with Lana Turner was a remake of The Rains Came *(1939). Burton played the Indian rajah.*
Who's Afraid of Virginia Woolf? (1966) was a battle of the sexes.
1984 (1984), with John Hurt as Winston Smith, was Burton's last movie.

Sean Connery

In the early 1960s the role of Ian Fleming's superspy James Bond was the biggest plum in filmdom. Several well known actors such as Richard Burton and James Mason were considered. But the role was finally given to a little known Scottish-born actor named Sean Connery, reportedly because the producers didn't have to pay him a fat salary.

Connery took the part and over a series of films built James Bond into one of the most popular characters in film history. During the 1960s when much of the film industry was in the doldrums, Connery's Bond films were surefire money-makers. Connery became an international superstar. But he was never really happy as James Bond.

The actor was born Thomas Connery on 25 August 1930 in Edinburgh, Scotland. He quit school at 15 to join the Navy and later worked a variety of jobs from lifeguard to coffin polisher. In his spare time he did body building, and he developed his physique to the point where he was able to get jobs as a model for swimming trunks. His well-muscled body also landed him a part in the London production of *South Pacific* – he was one of the chorus of sailors. After a year and a half in the chorus he went into repertory and began picking up a few small roles in minor films. He did better on TV, delivering some good solid dramatic performances, particularly in the BBC production of *Requiem for a Heavyweight*.

His impressive TV work got him a long term contract from 20th Century Fox. It seemed like a good deal at first, but it didn't turn out that way for Connery. He was loaned out to Disney for *Darby O'Gill and the Little People* (59), he played a supporting role in *Tarzan's Great Adventure* (60) and a private in *The Longest Day* (62). The former swimming trunks model and chorus boy was increasingly serious about acting, but increasingly frustrated by a career that didn't seem to be going anywhere. Then Bond came along.

The first of the Bond series was *Dr No* (63). Despite the enormous popularity of the Bond novels the film itself was not an immediate success. Reviews were bad. Critics said the stolid Connery was miscast as the suave spy. But the public seemed to warm to the film and while opening business was only fair, *Dr No* wound up to be one of the biggest moneymakers of the year.

The second and better Bond film, *From Russia With Love* (63) was even more popular, and by the third, *Goldfinger* (64) Sean Connery and James Bond had become a worldwide phenomenon, and Connery was the top male star in both the US and Britain. Yet when he stepped out of the Bond role he was not successful. He appeared in Alfred Hitchcock's *Marnie* (64), second-rate Hitchcock, second-rate Connery too.

He turned in a top flight and critically acclaimed performance in *The Hill* (65), a brutal and depressing film about an Army detention camp, which the public avoided. But as James Bond he could do no wrong and *Thunderball* (65), the fourth of the Bond series, was even bigger than the first three. While Connery was getting better in the role his identification with the Bond image became increasingly irritating, and he made his irritation public. To break the Bond sex-symbol image Connery appeared without his toupee in *Shalako* (69).

Connery was constantly renegotiating his contract, and finally the producers hired a new Bond – Australian George Lazenby, who made one unsuccessful Bond film.

Left: *As Ian Fleming's superspy James Bond, Sean Connery became a symbol of the swinging sixties. He has played Bond in six movies to date, five based on Fleming's thrillers, and the latest* Never Say Never Again *(1983).*

Above: In Zardoz (1974), Connery's role was that of a space-age bounty hunter.
Right: The Berber chieftain Raisuli was the hero of The Wind and the Lion (1975), a film set in turn-of-the-century North Africa.
Below: Part of the enjoyment of the Bond movies stemmed from the use of incredible devices and special effects.
Far right: In A Bridge Too Far (1977), Connery played the paratroop commander, Brigadier General Brian Urquhart.

Sean Connery was lured back once again for a reported $1,200,000 (most of which went to charity) and a chance to do some other films. The result, *Diamonds are Forever* (71), was the biggest and most popular Bond of all. But Connery was still unhappy and announced that he would never again play James Bond. Roger Moore was given the James Bond part, and proved to be extremely popular.

Connery went on to other things. One of them *The Anderson Tapes* (71), a taut and effective thriller, and his most successful non-Bond film to date. There were good adventure films like *The Man Who Would Be King* (75), based on the Rudyard Kipling short story. In 1976 Audrey Hepburn came out of semi-retirement to appear with Connery in *Robin and Marian*, and exciting, often touching, yet sadly unappreciated film. *Outland* (81) was a topnotch sci-fi adventure. There were also commercial and artistic failures like *The Next Man* (76) and *Meteor* (78) but in general Connery's reputation as an actor grew.

Still James Bond was always lurking in the background. In 1983 Connery came back for yet one more turn as agent 007, now grown middle aged. The film was appropriately titled *Never Say Never Again*. During that year the latest Moore Bond, *Octopussy*, was also released. It was the battle of the Bonds, and while both films did well, both the critics and the public agreed that Sean Connery was the better Bond.

Sean Connery: *No Road Back* 55, *Time Lock* 56, *Hell Drivers* 57, *Action of the Tiger* 57, *Another Time Another Place* 58, *Darby O'Gill and the Little People* 59, *Tarzan's Greatest Adventure* 59, *Frightened City* 59, *On the Fiddle* 61, *The Longest Day* 62, *Dr No* 62, *From Russia With Love* 63, *Woman of Straw* 64, *Marnie* 64, *Goldfinger* 64, *The Hill* 65, *Thunderball* 65, *A Fine Madness* 66, *You Only Live Twice* 67, *Shalako* 68, *The Molly Maguires* 69, *The Red Tent* 69, *The Anderson Tapes* 71, *Diamonds are Forever* 71, *The Offense* 72, *Zardoz* 74, *Ransom* 74, *Murder on the Orient Express* 74, *The Wind and the Lion* 75, *The Man Who Would Be King* 76, *Robin and Marian* 76, *The Next Man* 76, *A Bridge Too Far* 77, *The First Great Train Robbery* 78, *Meteor* 79, *Cuba* 80, *Time Bandits* 81, *Outland* 81, *Wrong is Right* 82, *Five Days of Summer* 82, *Never Say Never Again* 83.

Gary Cooper

T he only movie star to have a career like Gary Cooper is Gary Cooper. He was in motion pictures for 36 years, mostly at the top of the heap. Only three times in a span running from 1936 to 1957 did he miss the top ten money makers box office list. Winner of two Best Actor Academy Awards and an honorary Academy Award, Cooper also received high marks for his acting ability from such notable talents as John Barrymore, Charles Laughton and writer Graham Greene.

In the beginning of his career he co-starred with Clara Bow. By the end of his career it was Grace Kelly and Deborah Kerr. In Hollywood terms the distance between Bow and Kerr is measured in light years. Cooper was a star when Clark Gable was a nobody, and when Cary Grant was merely a gleam in Mae West's eye. So famous was Cooper (or Coop as he was called) that word went around Hollywood in the 30s that the name Cary Grant was a deliberate play on the name Gary Cooper, with Cary in place of Gary and the initials G C merely reversed to C G.

By the time of Cooper's death in 1961 his films had grossed an amazing two hundred million dollars and a television contest conducted by *Variety* seven years later showed his movies to be still popular. It's no accident then that when you're 'Puttin' on the Ritz' the guy to try to look like is a six foot-three, blue-eyed movie legend called Gary Cooper.

On 7 May 1901 Frank James Cooper was born in Helena, Montana. His parents were English but his father, a lawyer, eventually became a Montana State Supreme Court Justice. The family owned a 600-acre ranch. The Coopers returned to England with their children for several years but came back to America at the start of World War I. Frank worked on the family ranch and he worked hard. This would stand him in good stead later when he appeared in Westerns. No need for Cooper to learn a cowboy's skills, he knew them already.

Frank went to an agricultural school but a flair for drawing, particularly cartoons and caricatures, led him to Grinnell College in Iowa. He hoped for a career as a newspaper cartoonist. During the summers, he worked as a guide in Yellowstone National Park.

Cooper's father resigned from the bench lured by an opportunity to work in sunny California. Frank went along and tried hard to break into cartooning. Broke and getting nowhere he worked briefly as a door-to-door salesman for a local photographer and held other less than thrilling jobs. His prospects dim, Cooper decided to follow in the footsteps of several friends and try to find work as an extra in cowboy movies.

Back then extras in Westerns were basically stunt men. The same footage was used in a number of films so that even Cooper himself could never be quite sure what movies he was in. It's possible he appeared in as many as 50 films before audiences took to him in *The Winning of Barbara Worth* (26). By then he wasn't Frank anymore. He was Gary, after his agent's hometown, Gary, Indiana.

Cooper had an instinctive grasp of movie acting and the kind of low-key understated style the camera requires. He never had to readjust his technique the way stage trained actors do. Cooper served his 'theater' apprenticeship where it would do the most good, in reel after reel of film.

Cooper caught Clara Bow's eye with a two-scene bit in *It* (27), and he appeared with her in *Children of Divorce* (27),

---

Left: *Gary Cooper's last role, as the suspected murderer in* The Naked Edge *(1961), was a departure from the strong, silent heroes he had played since his first appearance in a B-Western called* The Thundering Herd *in 1925.*

Top: *Cooper with Mary Brien in* The Virginian *(1929), his first full talkie and the film which gave him his laconic reputation.*
Middle: *In* Northwest Mounted Police *(1940) with Madeleine Carroll and Robert Preston, Cooper played a Texas Ranger chasing a fugitive in Canada.*
Above: *Facing Cooper across the bar in* The Westerner *(1940) is Walter Brennan as the extraordinary Judge Roy Bean.*
Right: *Cooper as the heroic marshal, Will Kane, in* High Noon *(1952).*

a movie whipped into shape by a tirelessly demanding Joseph von Sternberg. Cooper and Bow were a twosome off-screen by then. His first starring role came in *Arizona Bound* (27). A small part in *Wings* (27) impressed the public and fan mail for Cooper began to arrive at Paramount. More Westerns followed, then a war movie with Fay Wray, *The Legion of the Condemned* (28). Cooper and Wray were described as 'Paramount's Glorious Young Lovers' by the publicity department, a phrase better applied to Wray and King Kong.

The Shopworn Angel (29) was a part talkie and Cooper sounded good. *The Virginian* (29) was his first full talkie, but ironically the dialogue consisted so heavily of 'yep' and 'nope' that Cooper won for ever the image of the strong silent type. By now Cooper was one of Paramount's leading romantic leads and an off-screen affair with the fiery Lupe Velez did him no harm at the box office. Cooper was boyish and charming in *Morocco* (30) with the new silver screen siren Marlene Dietrich, but Cooper felt von Sternberg was preoccupied with directing only Dietrich. He was happier with Rouben Mamoulian's direction of *City Streets* (31), a super moneymaker.

It was during the early 1930s that Gary Cooper discovered Europe's cafe society in all its glitter. He was a friend of Ernest Hemingway and later of the Duke and Duchess of Windsor. Abroad, his name was linked with the very rich Countess Dorothy di Frasso. But he came home (followed by the Countess) to make movies both for Paramount and on loan out. His *A Farewell to Arms* (32) with Helen Hayes was memorable. *Now and Forever* (34) boasted Carole Lombard and of all people, dimpled child star Shirley Temple. Mainly Cooper looked nervous.

The Lives of a Bengal Lancer (35) was his biggest picture to date. A splendid supporting cast, a good script and great action scenes make this one of the best adventure films ever. *Desire* (36) with Dietrich was a delicious little movie about the romance of a glamorous jewel thief and an American innocent. Though directed by Frank Borzage it was produced by Ernst Lubitsch and definitely had the Lubitsch touch.

In 1933 Cooper married a young socialite, Veronica 'Rocky' Balfe, whose one fling in pictures was being flung from a high building by gorilla King Kong. The scene never showed up in the finished movie. The Coopers had one child, a daughter Maria. Except for one brief period of separation in 1951 the marriage lasted until Cooper died.

Mr Deeds Goes to Town (36) won scads of awards and made a mint. Cooper played a simple country boy who proves he's better and wiser than all the city slickers put together. Cooper was in top form in the film and received his first Oscar nomination. *The Plainsman* (36), a Cecil B De Mille epic, was another huge success.

Studios fought to get Gary Cooper, star without peer, and since he had a good head for business he was never trapped by the studio system. By 1937 Gary Cooper was under contract to Samuel Goldwyn with Paramount getting first call on him for loan out. This odd arrangement was the result of a court case brought by Paramount. *Bluebeard's Eighth Wife* (38), for Paramount, with Claudette Colbert was a charming comedy.

The magnificent remake of a French Foreign Legion adventure picture *Beau Geste* (39), also for Paramount, helped make Gary Cooper not only the highest salaried actor in Hollywood but the top wage earner in America as well.

World War II changed the style of American movies and as with any change of direction not every star survived. Gary Cooper not only made the transition with ease but achieved his peak of popularity in the 1940s. Never a powerhouse of strength and stamina, Cooper was barred from military service because of his age and various ailments. Plagued with jaundice and anemia early in his career, he would later suffer from ulcers. Fortunately, his poor health didn't stand in his way when it came to making movies.

In *Sergeant York* (41), Cooper was outstanding as the country boy who moved from conscientious objector to war hero. The role brought Cooper his first Academy Award. He was Lou Gehrig in the finest of baseball movies, *The Pride of the Yankees* (42). He impressed audiences with his performance in *For Whom The Bell Tolls* (43) opposite Ingrid Bergman. Warner Brothers' *Saratoga Trunk* (45) was so popular the Gallup Poll of 1945 declared Gary Cooper America's favorite male star.

After the war Cooper free-lanced, never earning under $500,000 a year. In 1947 he testified before the House Committee on Un-American Activities. Politics aside, films of his testimony reveal a rare glimpse of Cooper not playing a part and his gestures are surprisingly effeminate considering his masculine movie image.

High Noon (52) brought Gary Cooper his second Oscar, deservedly, for he was wonderful as a brave sheriff left to face avenging killers on his own. Grace Kelly played his Quaker wife. Among his most notable later movies were *Vera Cruz* (54), a lively spoof of a Western; *Friendly Persuasion* (56), about an Indiana Quaker family during the Civil War; *Love in the Afternoon* (57) with Audrey Hepburn; *Man of the West* (58); *The Hanging Tree* (59); and *The Naked Edge* (61) with Deborah Kerr. Suffering through the final stages of cancer when he was awarded his honorary Oscar, Cooper had by then converted to Catholicism, the religious faith of his wife and daughter. On 13 May 1961, at the age of 60, he died.

Whether he played a Western hero or a light romantic lead Gary Cooper on screen was the embodiment of decency and integrity. He was America's ideal man, the man every woman wanted to marry and every man wanted to be. In his quiet way Coop was one of the best actors Hollywood ever produced.

Gary Cooper: *The Thundering Herd* 25, *Wild Horse Mesa* 25, *The Lucky Horseshoe* 25, *The Vanishing American* 25, *The Eagle* 25, *Tricks* 25, *Three Pals* 25, *Lightnin' Wins* 26, *The Enchanted Hill* 26, *Watch Your Wife* 26, *The Winning of Barbara Worth* 26, *It* 27, *Children of Divorce* 27, *Arizona Bound* 27, *Wings* 27, *Nevada* 27, *The Last Outlaw* 27, *Beau Sabreur* 28, *The Legion of the Condemned* 28, *Doomsday* 28, *Half a Bride* 28, *Lilac Time* 28, *The First Kiss* 28, *The Shopworn Angel* 29, *Wolf Song* 29, *Betrayal* 29, *The Virginian* 29, *Only The Brave* 30, *Paramount On Parade* 30, *The Texan* 30, *Seven Days Leave* 30, *A Man From Wyoming* 30, *The Spoilers* 30, *Morocco* 30, *Fighting Caravans* 31, *City Streets* 31, *I Take This Woman* 31, *His Woman* 31, *Make Me A Star* 32, *The Slippery Pearls* 32, *Voice of Hollywood* 32, *Devil and the Deep* 32, *If I Had a Million* 32, *A Farewell to Arms* 32, *Today We Live* 33, *One Sunday Afternoon* 33, *Design For Living* 33, *Alice in Wonderland* 33, *Operator 13* 33, *Now and Forever* 34, *The Wedding Night* 35, *Star Night at the Coconut Grove* 35, *The Lives of a Bengal Lancer* 35, *Peter Ibbetson* 35, *Desire* 36, *La Fiesta de Santa Barbara* 36, *Mr Deeds Goes to Town* 36, *Hollywood Boulevard* 36, *The General Died at Dawn* 36, *The Plainsman* 36, *Souls at Sea* 37, *Lest We Forget* 37, *The Adventures of Marco Polo* 38, *Bluebeard's Eighth Wife* 38, *The Cowboy and the Lady* 38, *Beau Geste* 39, *The Real Glory* 39, *The Westerner* 40, *North West Mounted Police* 40, *Meet John Doe* 40, *Sergeant York* 41, *Ball of Fire* 41, *The Pride of the Yankees* 42, *For Whom the Bell Tolls* 43, *The Story of Dr Wassell* 44, *Casanova Brown* 44, *Memo for Joe* 44, *Along Came Jones* 45, *Saratoga Trunk* 45, *Cloak and Dagger* 46, *Unconquered* 47, *Variety Girl* 47, *Good Sam* 48, *The Fountainhead* 48, *It's a Feeling* 49, *Snow Carnival* 49, *Task Force* 49, *Bright Leaf* 50, *Dallas* 50, *You're in the Navy Now* 51, *Starlift* 51, *It's a Big Country* 51, *Distant Drums* 51, *High Noon* 52, *Springfield Rifle* 52, *Return to Paradise* 53, *Blowing Wild* 53, *Garden of Evil* 54, *Vera Cruz* 54, *The Court-Martial of Billy Mitchell* 55, *Hollywood Mothers* 55, *Friendly Persuasion* 56, *Love in the Afternoon* 57, *Ten North Frederick* 58, *Man of the West* 58, *The Hanging Tree* 59, *Alias Jesse James* 59, *They Came to Cordura* 59, *The Wreck of the Mary Deare* 59, *The Naked Edge* 61.

Left top: In Morocco *(1930), Cooper played a Foreign Legionary bewitched by sensuous cabaret singer Marlene Dietrich.*
Left middle: Gary Cooper is recognized by Sterling Holloway (right) in Frank Capra's Meet John Doe *(1940).*
Left bottom: Pride of the Yankees *(1942), a film biography of baseball great Lou Gehrig, ended with Gehrig's emotional farewell in Yankee Stadium. In this locker room scene, Gehrig's fatal disease, a form of leukemia, becomes apparent.*
Right: As the determined General Mitchell, in The Court-Martial of Billy Mitchell *(1955), Cooper once again played a character who was willing to sacrifice everything, including reputation, to prove a point, in this case willful negligence on the part of the Army.*

James Dean

H e was either Jimmy (sounds like a kid) or James (suitably lofty for a legend), but he was never just plain Jim. His life was short; he never saw his twenty-fifth birthday. Yet he zoomed to stardom in a little over one year. With only three real films to his credit he became the greatest Hollywood legend since Rudolph Valentino. Hair cut short, a cigarette between his lips, jacket half unzipped to reveal the casual shirt underneath James Dean was a study of blue-jeaned informality. He wasn't conventionally handsome but he had an unusual and appealing face that expressed anger, pain, sensitivity and longing so well he drew audiences to him like a magnet. A hero to his generation and to all succeeding ones, Dean was a pace setter, a style creator, a symbol of alienated youth in a society where young and old are expected to conform and like it.

Born James Byron (fans like to think for the poet but most likely for a relative) Dean on 8 February 1931 in Marion, Indiana, he spent his early childhood in California. When his mother died, his father, a dental technician, sent the boy to live with family members in the heavily Quaker rural town of Fairmount, Indiana. Dean's life there appears to have been perfectly ordinary. He played on the high school basketball team. Taking sixth place in the State Dramatic Declamation Contest may have nudged Dean toward an acting career and after graduating from high school he went to UCLA.

Dean joined a drama group run by actor James Whitmore and got bit parts in four movies, *Fixed Bayonets* (51), *Sailor Beware* (51), *Has Anyone Seen My Gal?* (52) and *Trouble Along The Way* (53). Unhappy in California, Dean

moved to New York City, which he loved. When not working as a busboy and looking for acting jobs, he wrote poetry and painted pictures. But no matter how hard he tried to fit in, he was always a bit of a hayseed for New York, a young boy enamored with beat-generation novels and bongo drums.

A lot of live television came out of New York in the early 50s and Dean found roles on programs like 'The Kraft Television Theater,' 'The United States Steel Hour' and 'The Philco Television Playhouse.' He also found his way to the Actors' Studio where his talents really blossomed. His reputation for being moody and hard to get along with didn't prevent his getting a Broadway role in *See the Jaguar* with Arthur Kennedy in 1952. He played an Arab homosexual blackmailer in *The Immoralist*, based on Andre Gide's novel which ran on Broadway in 1954. Then came one of those miraculous theatrical moments when a star is born. Elia Kazan, impressed by his performance in *The Immoralist*, offered him the role of Cal in the movie version of John Steinbeck's novel, *East of Eden* (55). Dean stole the picture and became and overnight smash.

Dean was perfect as the bad boy every young girl would like to reform, the kid rejected by his father, the misfit waiting to be rescued, the genius who is a diamond in the rough. He went on to make *Rebel Without a Cause* (55) with Natalie Wood, and the JD (juvenile delinquent) became an American archetype rather than a worthless hood. Then Dean made *Giant* (56) directed by George Stevens with Elizabeth Taylor and Rock Hudson. He didn't like Stevens and the slick kinds of movies he made, but Dean was good as a cowhand who ages on film; the bad guy again but, as usual, a bad guy who gets the audience's sympathy.

On 9 September 1955, the day after James Dean completed *Giant*, he was killed in an auto accident driving his

Left: *James Dean is the eternal rebel, and a hero to rebellious youth everywhere. Almost 30 years after his death, he is still remembered; his three movies,* Rebel Without a Cause, East of Eden *and* Giant *are still watched with admiration.*

Above: *A tense moment in* Rebel Without a Cause *(1955) erupts as James Dean, the new boy in town, is goaded into a knife fight.*
Below: *James Dean confronts Julie Harris in Elia Kazan's adaptation of John Steinbeck's novel,* East of Eden *(1955). Dean's performance as the willful son trying to please his stern father brought him an Academy Award nomination.*

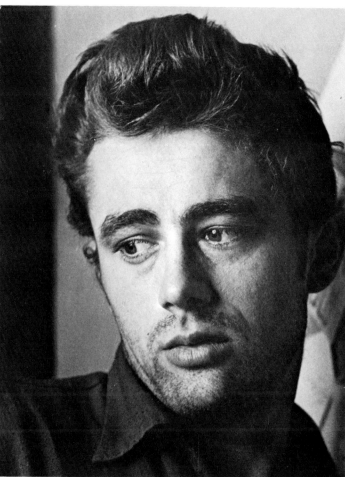

Left: *A publicity still of James Dean showing the sensitive features that have endeared him to generations of teenagers.*

Above: *James Dean as Jett Rink, the antagonist of* Giant *(1956) with Elizabeth Taylor, as Lesley Benedict, at his feet.*

brand new Porsche to Salinas to compete in a auto race. It was midnight for this Cinderella story. *Rebel Without a Cause* and *Giant* were released after his death. The reaction to Dean's death was, if anything, even more amazing than Dean's meteoric rise to success.

When James Dean died the Dean cult was born. His teenaged fans went crazy. They mobbed Fairmount, Indiana and made pilgrimages to his grave. They formed Dean clubs and collected memorabilia. There were Jimmy Dean look-alike contests all across America and some fans refused to believe he was dead, claiming he was in a nursing home and would return one day. Other Dean followers took up spiritualism to get in touch with him 'beyond the grave,' or believed they were reincarnations of the actor. Books were written about Dean; he was canonized in poems, songs and plays. His films made such a mint that his studio, Warner Brothers, put together a documentary

called *The James Dean Story* (57). The cult spread beyond American to Europe and points beyond.

The legend is alive today. James Dean is still popular. Teenagers who consider their parent's generation positively prehistoric put Dean posters up on their wall as if 1955 were yesterday. In a sense they're right because James Dean, sullen, sexy, an incipient rebel, was ahead of his time. He pointed the way to the 1960s when the young would give their love, not to movie stars, but to rock stars.

James Dean really belongs to the timeless world of the Beatles, the Rolling Stones and David Bowie rather than to Hollywood of the 1950s. No wonder Elvis Presley revered him.

James Dean: *Fixed Bayonets* 51, *Sailor Beware* 51, *Has Anybody Seen My Gal?* 52, *Trouble Along the Way* 53, *East of Eden* 55, *Rebel Without a Cause* 55, *Giant* 56.

Clint Eastwood

In 1971 *Life* magazine ran this line on its front cover: 'The world's favorite movie star is – no kidding – Clint Eastwood.' The title was accurate. More than a decade later Eastwood could still stake a solid claim to the title of 'world's favorite movie star.' He is certainly the most highly paid.

His record of box office success is unequalled by any living actor. Practically every film in which he has appeared has made *Variety's* annual chart of the biggest box-office hits. Eastwood has achieved this remarkable record entirely on his own. He has produced many of the films in which he has appeared, and directed some. He has succeeded without a major studio buildup, and, in the view of his detractors, without any real acting talent.

Most Eastwood films are panned by the major film critics. He has never won an Academy Award. He has never even been nominated. Yet in 1980 when a TV show called *People's Choice Award* conducted a massive telephone survey to find the most popular actors in America Eastwood came out on top and received the first Life Achievement Award. Clint Eastwood is more than a superstar, he is a genuine phenomenon.

There is absolutely nothing in Eastwood's early life that would lead one to predict such a career. He was born on 31 May 1930 in San Francisco. It was the depression and his father had a tough time finding and holding a job. The family traveled all over the West with Clint rarely spending more than a semester in any one school. Yet he was no rebel à la Brando. He was always a good if not brilliant student. Clint appeared in one high school play – a disaster, he recalls. He was more interested in athletics and he

became a basketball star of sorts because he was taller than most of the other students.

After graduation Clint drifted around working at a variety of jobs from lifeguard to lumberjack. He was drafted just in time for the Korean war, but spent his army career teaching swimming at Fort Ord, California. After the army he enrolled in business administration at Los Angeles City College, married Maggie Johnson, a girl he had met on a blind date, and picked up what part time work he could. His life was remarkably unremarkable.

Some of Eastwood's friends persuaded him that he was good looking enough to try out for the movies so he took a screen test at Universal. He photographed well and got a contract that guaranteed him 40 weeks work at $75 a week. It has been said that he appeared in 14 early films, but he must have been only a face in a crowd in most of them. He only got screen credit for seven, and his part was generally so small that if you blinked you missed him. He got a reasonably decent part in a perfectly lousy western *Ambush at Cimarron Pass* (58).

Eastwood's film career was hardly prospering. He supplemented his modest income by doing bit parts on television and on a chance visit to CBS-TV in New York in 1958 he was spotted and picked for the second lead in a new Western series, *Rawhide*.

Rawhide was Eastwood's first major break. His second came in 1964 when he got an offer from Italian director Sergio Leone to do, of all things a Western, to be shot in Spain. Italian film companies were making money filming low budget quickies dubbed 'spaghetti Westerns'. The cast was usually European - though names were sometimes anglicized in the credits for effect. Often an American actor (though never a high-priced star) was hired to play the lead. That was Eastwood's position in the film ultimately called *A Fistful of Dollars* (64). His character was

The Man With No Name, a drifter and loner who remorselessly and unemotionally (though sometimes sadistically) slaughters large numbers of people. He is somewhat better than the bad guys in the film – but not much. Eastwood played the part wrapped in a seedy poncho with a battered sombrero, a scrubby beard and a black cheroot clenched between his teeth.

Eastwood never thought this film would be the turning point in his career until months later he read in *Variety* that the picture had become a fantastic success in Italy and he got a letter from the producer about making a second in the series. It was *For a Few Dollars More* (65) and it made not just a few dollars but millions. Eastwood put on the poncho as The Man With No Name one more time in *The Good, the Bad and the Ugly* (66), the most expensively made, most sadistic and most successful of the Eastwood-Leone collaborations. America and Britain had to wait to see these films because a Japanese film company was suing the producers claiming – correctly – that *Fistful* was a direct steal from the Japanese samurai classic *Yojimbo*. In the meantime Hollywood, sensing a trend, hired Eastwood for *Hang 'Em High* (68), a Western every bit as brutal as the *Dollar* trilogy. All four films hit the American market at about the same time and in 1968 Clint Eastwood was 5th on the US box office list.

As a major star Eastwood was now able to take his choice of roles. Sometimes he made a mistake, as in the musical *Paint Your Wagon* (69). The kindest thing that could be said about his performance is that he sang better than co-star Lee Marvin. The film still made money. *The Beguiled* (71), an almost gothic horror tale, was not a popular success, though some fans consider it one of his best films. In general however, an Eastwood film meant a steady flow of cash at the box office.

Above: *In* The Outlaw Josey Wales *(1976), Eastwood played a rancher seeking out and killing the band of outlaws responsible for the death of his wife.*
Left: The Enforcer *(1976), co-starring Tyne Daly, featured Eastwood as 'Dirty' Harry Callaghan for the third time.*
Top right: *Clint Eastwood as 'The Man With No Name' in the famous spaghetti western* For A Few Dollars More *(1965). This film, like its predecessor,* For A Fistful of Dollars, *was directed by Italian Sergio Leone.*
Right: Hang 'em High *(1968) was the first western made in Hollywood to imitate the brutality and gore of the spaghetti westerns. It was as successful as it was bloody.*

Eastwood made his debut as a director in *Play Misty for Me* (71), a Hitchcock-like thriller in which he also starred. *Misty* did well at the box office and attracted surprisingly good reviews. Eastwood got his favorite director Don Segal to take a small part acting in the film.

But Eastwood's big film of 1971 was *Dirty Harry*, in which he plays a cop who would not hesitate to take the law into his own hands. The film aroused a storm of controversy, with many critics saying it celebrated police-state tactics. The public loved it and *Dirty Harry* quickly outgrossed any of Eastwood's previous films. He returned as Harry Callahan in several other films, but softened Harry's vigilante image somewhat.

Left: *Beauty and the Beast – Clint Eastwood has co-starred with Clyde in two movies,* Any Which Way But Loose *(1978) and* Any Which Way You Can *(1980).*
Below: *In a change of pace World War II-adventure, Eastwood, seen here with Ingrid Pitt, played a member of an Allied paratroop commando group who parachute into a German fortress in the thriller* Where Eagles Dare *(1969).*
Bottom right: *The archetypal Eastwood hero is an American favorite.*

The most popular of all the films in Clint Eastwood's remarkable career is *Every Which Way but Loose* (78). It has been called a 'redneck comedy' and his co-star was an appealing orang-utan named Clyde. Eastwood and the ape teamed up again in *Any Which Way You Can* (80).

Even those who dismiss Eastwood's acting ability recognize that he is an extremely hard working professional who has no time for temperament and hates the waste of time or money on the set. For a star his private life is extremely private. His long-time marriage ended quietly in divorce. His relationship with actress Sondra Locke has been the subject of rumors, but the gossips have been given very little to chew on. He rarely grants interviews or makes public appearances. If fans want Clint Eastwood they have to see his films. Millions do.

Clint Eastwood: *Revenge of the Creature 55, Francis in the Navy 55, Lady Godiva 55, Never Say Goodbye 56, The First Traveling Saleslady 56, Star in the Dust 56, Escapade in Japan 57, Ambush in Cimarron Pass 58, Lafayette Escadrille 58, A Fistful of Dollars 64, For a Few Dollars More 65, The Good, the Bad and the Ugly 66, The Witches 67, Hang 'Em High 68, Coogan's Bluff 68, Where Eagles Dare 69, Paint Your Wagon 69, Kelly's Heroes 70, Two Mules for Sister Sara 70, The Beguiled 70, Play Misty for Me 71, Dirty Harry 71, Joe Kidd 72, High Plains Drifter 73, Magnum Force 73, Thunderbolt and Lightfoot 74, The Eiger Sanction 75, The Outlaw Josey Wales 76, The Enforcer 76, The Gauntlet 77, Every Which Way but Loose 78, Escape from Alcatraz 79, Bronco Billy 80, Any Which Way You Can 80, Firefox 82, Honkey Tonk Man 83, Sudden Impact 84, Tightrope 84.*

Errol Flynn

There's a playful ring to the name Errol Flynn and to a great extent this hero of swashbuckling romance lived up to his name. But unlike a costume picture, his life did not have a happy ending.

He was born in Hobart, Tasmania, in 1909. Flynn's father, Professor Theodore Thomson Flynn, was a marine biologist and zoologist whose contributions to his field ultimately won him an MBE (Member of the British Empire). Son Errol was very different. A boxer, a swimmer, a natural allround athlete, he was a disastrously poor student. Though he was sent to very fine schools in Australia and England, it was really no use. Flynn would get by in life on his good looks, dashing manner, and almost magical charm.

It is hard to know precisely what Errol Flynn did between his schoolboy years and the start of his movie career. Blessed with the gift of gab he was a most engaging liar. According to Flynn he spent his early years as an adventurer who worked passage on ships, was an overseer on a copra plantation, ran a charter schooner, smuggled diamonds and hunted tropical birds. Flynn was a daring sort who loved the sea and who was usually either in trouble or barely skirting it, so some of his stories are probably true. One fact, though, is established, He spent 1926 working as a shipping clerk in Sydney, Australia.

However he spent his time thereafter he surfaced in 1933 in an Australian movie, *In the Wake of the Bounty* (33). Since there wasn't much work for actors in Australia, Flynn went to England, where he spent a year and a half with the Northampton Repertory Company.

Flynn's first real break came when he landed the lead in *Murder in Monte Carlo* (34), a film made at Warner Brothers' Teddington Studio. The movie was his ticket to Hollywood. He arrived there at the beginning of 1935 and by the end of 1935 he was a star.

Flynn met his first wife, French film star Lili Damita, on the boat to America. The couple had one child, a son Sean, who had a brief career in French and Spanish movies in the 1960s. The Flynn-Damita match was, to say the least, rocky. Errol Flynn's escapades with women were wild, public and numerous. No one except his wives, apparently, ever took him to be a family man.

Epic swashbucklers had been popular during the silent film era when Douglas Fairbanks ruled the screen. After sound came in, movie audiences were so intrigued with dialogue that big splashy costume pictures relying mostly on visual imagery disappeared. By 1935 Warner's, sensing a revival of the genre, decided to make Rafael Sabatini's 1922 novel *Captain Blood* into a movie with Robert Donat. At the last minute Donat bowed out. The sets were built, everything was in readiness. Desperately, Warner's cast about for a lead who could start work fast. Enter contract player Errol Flynn, eager and handsome.

The heretofore unknown Flynn played the pirate/hero in *Captain Blood* (35) magnificently. What's more, Flynn and his co-star Olivia de Havilland clicked on screen. Her restraint and his flamboyance struck just the right note with audiences. Flynn and de Havilland would be teamed seven more times until de Havilland won her battle to play more demanding roles. Nobody took costume romances seriously, even good ones. The low reputation of swashbucklers as a film category was painful to Errol Flynn but it was a view he shared. It's too bad he did because he wound up denigrating his very real achievements.

Left: *As the dashing and ambitious Robert Devereaux, Earl of Essex, Errol Flynn starred with Bette Davis in* The Private Lives of Elizabeth and Essex *(1939). He was one of the few stars who actually looked well in sixteenth-century dress.*

Above: *As Peter Blood, the doctor sentenced to deportation for aiding the wounded in Monmouth's Rebellion, Errol Flynn had his first starring role, though the part had been written for Robert Donat.*
Right: *The Charge of the Light Brigade (1936) was the perfect vehicle for Flynn's heroics. Set in India and the Crimea, it was the story of two brothers in love with the same girl. Flynn actually gave up Olivia de Havilland to Patric Knowles.*

Years later when Olivia de Havilland saw reissued versions of the movies she'd made with Flynn she was astonished at how well they held up and how utterly delightful they were. They put to shame many 'important' movies of the era. Flynn had no rival when it came to acrobatic grace or witty delivery of even the most banal dialogue. Whereas most actors had to work like the dickens to learn swordplay Errol Flynn picked it up instantly.

1936 to 1942 were Flynn's peak years when he dominated the screen, the news, and the hearts of millions of women. Jack Warner called him a 'magnificent sexy animal package.' He also revealed another side to himself, a knack for writing. Flynn's book, the autobiographical *Beam Ends* came out in 1937. It wasn't his first venture in this direction. He'd done columns on New Guinea life for The Sydney *Bulletin* before he went to England. His last memoir, *My Wicked Wicked Ways*, written in collaboration with well-known ghost-writer Earl Conrad, was published posthumously in 1959.

Flynn always complained that he was typecast but a glance at his films shows he really wasn't. He was a British officer in *The Charge of the Light Brigade* (36), an idealistic young surgeon in *Green Light* (37), which was a modern film, not a costume drama. He was back in costume again for *The Prince and the Pauper* (37). *Another Dawn* (37), a soap opera of a film, had Flynn as a cricket and polo-playing type. The score, written by Erich Wolfgang Korngold was so beautiful the composer used it again in a violin concerto he wrote for Jascha Heifetz years later. Flynn did a charming comedy, *The Perfect Specimen* (37), which he certainly was.

The Adventures of Robin Hood (38), perhaps his most famous film, followed. It differed markedly from Douglas Fairbanks's 1922 silent movie, *Robin Hood*, but it established Flynn as Fairbanks's unparalleled successor. Flynn, looking glorious in tights, leaped, vaulted, fenced and wooed like a champ. The movie, which borrowed rather freely from Sir Walter Scott's *Ivanhoe*, cost a record two million dollars to make and was worth every penny. Warner's used a new three-color Technicolor process and the movie looked beautiful. It was a super smash, well reviewed, with Flynn and de Havilland in top form, making it the first (animated films aside) great technicolor success. Reissued in 1948 it was a success again.

Four's a Crowd (38) was a screwball comedy. *The Sisters*

(38) was really a Bette Davis vehicle but Flynn insisted and got top billing. She didn't like him, whether for that or something else, and later when they were under consideration as possible candidates for Scarlett and Rhett in *Gone With The Wind* she rebelled.

The Dawn Patrol (38) about the 59th Squadron of the British Royal Flying Corps during World War I, and *Dodge City* (39), a Western followed. That was the year Errol Flynn made the box office top ten in America and Britain, holding a spot on the British list even after he lost it in America. Like it or not, Davis got him again in *The Private Lives of Elizabeth and Essex* (39).

Virginia City (40) came next. Flynn is the only British actor Americans would accept as a star in Hollywood Westerns. He used to joke about this, describing himself as 'the rich man's Roy Rogers.' Audiences liked him best swashing and buckling but they were glad to see him with a six-gun in hand, too.

The Sea Hawk (40), one of Flynn's best, was based loosely on the exploits of Sir Francis Drake. A splendid adventure film, it boasted as script revisor Howard Koch whose radio writing included Orson Welles's famous *War of the Worlds* broadcast of 1938. Unlike *The Adventures of Robin Hood*, where Flynn did most of his own stunts and duelling, the big duel to the death scene in *The Sea Hawk* was doubled, perhaps because of his poor health.

Above: *Flynn was never better than in* The Adventures of Robin Hood *(1938). A Hollywood milestone for its use of color, it had an all-star cast, including Olivia de Havilland as Maid Marian and Basil Rathbone as the evil Sir Guy of Gisborne.*

Below: *One of the great duels in* The Sea Hawk *(1940), a movie set in the reign of Elizabeth I. Flynn played a captain famed for his exploits against the Spanish. His chief opponent was the crafty Spanish Ambassador played by Claude Rains.*

Errol Flynn's 'live two lives in one' style of getting through the world was catching up with him. Though his dashing style and Warner's power in Tinseltown got him out of most scrapes, there were night club brawls aplenty. Flynn's drinking was way up and his discipline on the set way down. What's more, his looks were going, and he was about to lose his leading co-star. His last film with de Havilland was *They Died With Their Boots On* (41), a title that led to many jokes when Flynn was brought to trial for statutory rape. He was acquitted, but the trial was a publicist's comic dream, what with one of the underage girls claiming Flynn assaulted her as she gazed at the moon through the porthole of his boat, *Sirocco*. Working at the cigar counter at the Los Angeles Hall of Justice during the rape trial was a pretty teenaged girl (Flynn liked them young, very young) whose father worked for the sheriff. Flynn saw her, liked her, and married her. The whole thing sounds like a screwball comedy. It even brought back to common usage the old expression, 'In like Flynn.'

When war broke out in Europe, Errol Flynn became an American citizen to avoid serving in the British or Australian Army. He did try to enlist in the US Army later but was declared 4F for medical reasons. He didn't suffer at the box office because of the rape trial, as Warner's had feared, and he made several war movies, including *Objective, Burma!* (45), in which Flynn was particularly good. The movie was withdrawn from British cinemas because it was presumed to glorify America's part in the Burma invasion at the expense of Britain. His postwar films revealed a new Flynn image. He was sometimes seedy; he could even be menacing. His reputation as a libertine was catching up with him on screen.

The Adventures of Don Juan (48) restored some of Flynn's former glory. His drinking was a major problem during filming and he was forced to play the fool a bit, spoofing himself, but it's a rollicking movie which did well, especially in Europe, but apparently not well enough. Warner's, sensitive to the bottom line, reduced the budget on all future Flynn films.

Loaned to MGM he made *That Forsyte Woman* (49) with Greer Garson, based on John Galsworthy's trilogy, *The Forsyte Saga*. Behaving responsibly on the set, Flynn presented an interesting characterization of Soames Forsyte and he was justly proud of his performance.

Flynn tried his hand at co-producing films with disastrous results. He lost every penny on an ill-fated attempt to make *William Tell*, but was saved from financial ruin by English producer-director Herbert Wilcox who signed Flynn to play opposite popular British performer Anna Neagle in *Lilacs in the Spring* (54), and *King's Rhapsody* (55). Flynn's third and last wife, starlet Patrice Wymore, played the ingenue in *King's Rhapsody*. His career received an upward jolt when he played Mike Campbell in *The Sun Also Rises* (57), based on the Ernest Hemingway novel. He received excellent reviews. He was good as a screen drunk in *Too Much Too Soon* (58), the film version of Diana Barrymore's autobiography, and in John Huston's *The Roots of Heaven* (58).

But he was much too far down now ever to climb back up. A drug addict, an alcoholic, a chain smoker, Flynn had also suffered through bouts of malaria. He'd had tuberculosis, gonorrhea, and by the end he had acute hepatitis. Unable even to remember lines, he was suspended by Actors Equity when he tried to return to the stage. He died in 1959 of a heart attack.

It's best to remember him in his prime, nimbly scrambling up a vine to whisper sweet nothings to a fair maiden or at sword points ready to dispatch a villain. He lived fully, recklessly, like a soldier of fortune. People adored him. Never has any man been forgiven debts, faults, infidelities, and maybe even larceny the way Errol Flynn was. In the movie *My Favorite Year* Peter O'Toole played a character based on Errol Flynn. O'Toole's 'Flynn' was a lovable irresponsible man who could charm the birds out of the trees. O'Toole was right; practically nobody could resist Errol Flynn.

Errol Flynn: *In the Wake of the Bounty* 33, *Murder at Monte Carlo* 34, *The Case of the Curious Bride* 35, *Don't Bet on Blondes* 35, *Captain Blood* 35, *The Charge of the Light Brigade* 36, *Green Light* 37, *The Prince and the Pauper* 37, *Another Dawn* 37, *The Perfect Specimen* 37, *The Adventures of Robin Hood* 38, *Four's a Crowd* 38, *The Sisters* 38, *The Dawn Patrol* 38, *Dodge City* 39, *The Private Lives of Elizabeth and Essex* 39, *Virginia City* 40, *The Sea Hawk* 40, *Santa Fe Trail* 40, *Footsteps in the Dark* 41, *Dive Bomber* 41, *They Died with their Boots On* 41, *Desperate Journey* 42, *Gentleman Jim* 42, *Edge of Darkness* 43, *Thank Your Lucky Stars* 43, *Northern Pursuit* 43, *Uncertain Glory* 44, *Objective, Burma!* 45, *San Antonio* 45, *Never Say Goodbye* 46, *Cry Wolf* 47, *Escape Me Never* 47, *Silver River* 48, *The Adventures of Don Juan* 48, *It's a Great Feeling* 49, *That Forsyte Woman* 49, *Montana* 50, *Rocky Mountain* 50, *Kim* 51, *Hello God* 51, *The Adventures of Captain Fabian* 51, *Mara Maru* 52, *Against All Flags* 52, *Cruise of the Zaca* 52, *The Master of Ballantrae* 53, *Crossed Swords* 54, *Lilacs in the Spring* 55, *The Warriors* 55, *King's Rhapsody* 55, *Istanbul* 56, *The Big Boodle* 57, *The Sun Also Rises* 57, *Too Much, Too Soon* 58, *The Roots of Heaven* 58, *Cuban Rebel Girls* 59.

Right: *Flynn's military service was spent making films like* Objective Burma! *(1945). Such pictures were considered great propaganda.*
Far left: *As Mike Campbell, one of the Lost Generation in* The Sun Also Rises *(1957), Flynn gave one of the best performances of his later career. Others in the cast included (left to right) Ava Gardner, Mel Ferrer, Tyrone Power and Eddie Albert.*
Below: *As General George Armstrong Custer at the Battle of the Little Big Horn in* They Died With Their Boots On *(1941). Somehow, Tasmanian-born Flynn was utterly believable when playing a completely American hero like Custer.*

Clark Gable

Clark Gable was tall, dark and handsome. Silent film stars had been a romantic lot, with soulful eyes, apt to send a lady flowers. Not Gable. He was king of a new breed of Hollywood heroes popularized by the talkies, more comfortable flinging wise-cracks at a woman than flowers. Gable had jug-size ears, dimples, an impudent self-mocking grin and a way of sweeping movie heroines off their feet which made them seem light as a feather. Big, sexy, and every inch a he-man from the balls of his feet to his jet-black hair, Gable was nonetheless a classy gent. You'd never catch him crushing a grapefruit in a lady's face.

Clark Gable was his real name and he was born in Cadiz, Ohio, in 1901. His mother died when he was a baby, a situation which led to endless psychoanalytic speculation in fan magazines once the baby grew up. Because Gable had many love affairs and several marriages, gossip columnists were forever accusing him of trying to find a replacement for his mother. The simple fact that women lusted after Gable in droves never seemed explanation enough.

Gable was raised by his stepmother. She encouraged him to read books and listen to music. Gable's father was a tough macho type who hated 'sissies.' By sissies he meant actors, musicians and even readers. So Gable left home and father in his teens, working long and hard as a laborer. He knew what it was to be broke and memories of poverty would haunt him even when he lived in the lap of luxury.

Somewhere along the way Gable discovered vaudeville and fell in love with acting. He joined a down-at-heels,

barely professional acting company which was trying to survive by touring. Gable took his roles seriously but grave doubts about his talent hampered him. He never overcame these insecurities, considering himself a personality rather than an actor throughout his entire career, no matter what the critics or his fans said. Gable wound up in California where he met Josephine Dillon, a drama coach 14 years his senior. Now Gable may have underestimated his appeal as an actor but his sex appeal was never in question. He became Josephine Dillon's protegé and husband. She wasn't the first woman to fall for him and help him and she wouldn't be the last.

In the mid 1920s Gable was an extra in a few films, but that was all. On the stage however, things picked up for him, especially when he appeared in Houston. There Gable met a wealthy Texas divorcée who would become his second wife. She was 17 years older than he was. Gable tried Hollywood again but he bombed out on screen tests for MGM and Warners. Still, it was a new era. Sound had arrived. Gable persevered. He finally got to play a heavy in a Pathé western, *The Painted Desert* (31). Studios that had spurned him looked again. He was photogenic and charismatic. MGM, considering him a natural gangster type, gave him a contract. He would remain an MGM contract player for the bulk of his career and thanks to him MGM made a fortune. He made *Dance Fools Dance* (31) with the famous and glamorous Joan Crawford. Sparks didn't fly between them yet. Gable was still unknown. But the day came when Crawford saw Gable as the epitome of movie manhood, on screen and off. *A Free Soul* (31) made Gable a star. He played a bad guy badly used by Norma Shearer who got his own back by shoving her around. Audiences could see she only wanted him for the sex. But what sex! MGM was beseiged with fan letters.

Left: *Clark Gable in his best known role, that of the dashing, blockade runner Rhett Butler in* Gone With The Wind *(1939). Seen here with Vivien Leigh as Scarlett O'Hara, Gable was the only actor truly considered for the part.*

Laughing Sinners (31), again with Crawford, and a starring role in Sporting Blood (31), got him launched. He was chosen over the fading John Gilbert for Susan Lennox: Her Fall and Rise (31), with the illustrious Garbo. The by now overworked Gable learned a lot about handling the studio big shots by watching Garbo. Someday he, too, would have a 9-5 work day written into his contract. Possessed (31), with Joan Crawford was followed by a big one, Hell's Divers (31), with Wallace Beery, whose salary Gable envied.

By now Clark Gable had established himself as a man's man as well as a ladies' man. He liked to hunt and fish. He was a good mechanic, a skill he never lost. He could hold his liquor and he enjoyed the company of men. During the Depression years when the whole USA went to the movies, his audience seemed to consist of everybody in the country.

Red Dust (32), with platinum blonde Jean Harlow, was one of his best films. It was the classic triangle with Gable chasing a prim and rather dull Mary Astor while the tart and curvy Jean Harlow chased him. Gable and Harlow were so much fun together it was a match only Heaven or Hollywood could have made. The ending, where Harlow reads a dopey kid's story to the bed-ridden Gable while his hand creeps slowly up her leg, is movie legend. Red Dust shot Gable on to Hollywood's top ten moneymakers list. He stayed there, rarely falling below second place until he enlisted in the Army Air Corps in World War II and temporarily quit making movies.

Above: Clark Gable as Fletcher Christian faces Charles Laughton as the inhuman Captain Bligh in the first version of Mutiny on the Bounty (1935).

He made No Man of Her Own at Paramount with Carole Lombard (32), but their romance was still down the road. Hold Your Man (33) teamed him with Harlow again. Night Flight (33) gave him Helen Hayes and Myrna Loy to work with. It was Crawford again in Dancing Lady (33). So far so good. Crawford and Loy were strong types, nice foils for Gable. But his best 'little picture' was yet to come.

Gable had been pushing MGM for more money and better roles so Louis B Mayer decided to punish him for it. Gable and Mayer never did get along. Gable (who, unknown to the public, wore at least a partial plate of false teeth) used to threaten to throw his teeth through Mayer's window, aiming for his head. The punishment Mayer decreed for Gable was making a movie called It Happened One Night (34) at a poverty-row studio, Columbia Pictures. The thing was meant to bomb at the box office. It was hard to find a female lead. At last a reluctant Claudette Colbert agreed to make the film if her terms were met. Frank Capra directed the movie and, maybe because nobody took it seriously, the cast wound up having a good time. Their playful spirit bubbled over to audiences when the film was released. It Happened One Night was one of the best movies of the era, taking the Academy Award for Best Picture and winning Oscars for Colbert and Gable, too. Columbia made a fortune. MGM gave Gable a raise. The only losers, unless we count Louis B Mayer, were underwear manufacturers. Gable wore no undershirt in the movie because he thought he would look awkward stripping it off when he had to bare his chest. American men figured if Gable didn't wear an undershirt no man should. Undershirt sales tumbled.

Gable's luck held and he continued to prove pure gold. Appearing with Crawford, Loy, Constance Bennett and Loretta Young, Gable made film after film that was hot box office. *China Seas* (35) was the best of the lot. It was Harlow again with Rosalind Russell tossed in as the aristocrat who loses to the tart. Gable balked at doing *Mutiny on the Bounty* (35). Ever modest, he thought Charles Laughton's Captain Bligh would steal the picture. But Gable was a good Fletcher Christian. He brought a solid masculinity to the role and kept the character from being namby-pamby virtuous. *San Francisco* (36) had Gable playing a heroic saloon keeper whose mocking manner hides deep love. This time the love was directed toward Jeanette MacDonald. Spencer Tracy was also in the movie. Gable admired Tracy's talent but considered it a threat. Audiences, however, thought they made a great team. *San Francisco* ended with an earthquake that caused an explosion at the box office. It made big bucks.

In 1937 Gable and Loy were chosen king and queen of Hollywood, based on a newspaper poll. They received tin crowns. It was a gala event and Gable's title stuck. Ironically, his next movie, *Parnell* (37), was a flop. Both he and Loy were panned by the critics and the public agreed. Gable was making *Saratoga* (37) with Harlow when she died. Her death stunned Gable and rocked the nation. A young woman named Mary Dees, posing with her back to the camera, finished the film in Harlow's place. This ghoulish piece of ghost acting did nothing to hurt the picture's success. Audiences mobbed theaters to catch one last necrophilic glimpse of Harlow. *Test Pilot* (37), with Tracy and Loy, was one of the hottest pictures of the year.

Gable went on enriching MGM but there was talk of a movie so major it would put everything else he'd done in the shade. David O Selznick owned the rights to Margaret Mitchell's huge best seller *Gone With The Wind* and he wanted just the right cast for the movie. Every female in Tinseltown this side of Lassie tried to get the part of Scarlett O'Hara. Vivien Leigh won. But there was only one serious contender for Rhett Butler. To get Gable, Selznick had to do much wheeling and dealing with Louis B Mayer. After two years of shenanigans he was able to assemble his cast. Though Gable received the part of Rhett practically by public acclamation, he was miserable. All his old insecurities had returned to bedevil him. But he made a perfect Rhett Butler. His 'Frankly, my dear, I don't give a damn' broke a Hollywood tabu against swearing and gave a delicious shock to the multitudes. The lavish and spectacularly expensive *Gone With The Wind* (39) became one of the top grossing pictures of all time. Gable's salary was raised to $7500 a week, a princely sum in the depression but a mere pittance compared to the movie's profits, in which Gable had no share. MGM acquired Selznick's interest in *Gone With The Wind* in 1942, subsequently making millions. Yet the studio's fabled Rhett Butler received not one extra penny when the movie was

Above: *Gable sychronizes watches with those involved in the bombing of Germany in* Command Decision *(1949).*
Below: *With the carefully applied dust of the earthquake of* San Francisco *(1936) still upon him, Gable takes a tea-break on the set. Jeanette MacDonald and Spencer Tracy co-starred.*

reissued. For the rest of his life an embittered Gable felt that his one chance to be really rich had gone with the wind.

To the dazzling premiere of the film in Atlanta, Gable brought his new bride, Carole Lombard. She wasn't in his league when it came to stardom but she was a beautiful, brilliant and gifted comedienne. She was also rich, something she achieved all on her own, by the clever way she managed her career. A generous madcap, she had an exhibitionist's eye for publicity. There were rumors aplenty about the couple but Gable adored her. The ranch he lived on with Carole remained his home till the day he died.

Boom Town (40), *Comrade X* (40), with Hedy Lamarr, *Honky Tonk* (41) and *Somewhere I'll Find You* (42), with Lana Turner, showed the Gable box office magic was still intact despite a new kind of Hollywood born with the war. The 1940s ushered in patriotic sentimental films, message pictures, to comfort and spur on the homefront. World War II took its toll of Clark Gable early. Carole Lombard became one of the war's casualties. In 1942, flying home from a tour to sell war bonds, the plane she was on crashed into a rock cliff. The war had blacked out beacons that might have guided the plane. Gable mourned. He would marry again later, first Lady Sylvia Ashley, and finally Kay Spreckles who bore Gable a son he never lived to see. In the meantime there was the war and his personal grief. He was 41 when he joined up. In 1942 he was assigned to a base north of London. Gable never tried to sit out the war. He flew bombing missions. The Germans even offered a special reward to anyone who could bring him in.

After the war, word went round that 'Gable's back and Garson's got him.' He made *Adventure* with her (45). But some of his old sparkle was gone. Perhaps this was because his war record forced Hollywood to canonize him, robbing him of his irreverent charm. Perhaps it was the studio itself. By the 1950s MGM was in trouble. The days of the studio system were on their way out. Dore Schary, MGM's new head, suspended Gable, and in 1953 the studio went so far as to refuse to renew his contract. The day Clark Gable left MGM there was no last hurrah or fond farewell for the one-time king, which must have stung. But Gable was still king and his career far from over. He made *Mogambo*, (53), a new version of *Red Dust*, with Ava Gardner and Grace Kelly. John Huston directed and the film was a gem. Gable and Kelly, true pros, worked hard and did some sightseeing together in Africa where the movie was filmed. *Mogambo* was a hit and MGM offered him a new and very sweet deal. Gable didn't take it, signing with 20th Century Fox instead. A western, *The Tall Men* (55), proved he was still a hot property.

But time was passing and Gable showed wear and tear. He drank more. He developed tremors. Even his head shook, a problem in close-ups. He tried forming his own company. He did some comedies for Paramount. But he needed something special, something worthy of his status.

Along came *The Misfits* (61) written by Arthur Miller for his wife Marilyn Monroe. The cast included Montgomery Clift as well as Gable. It was a moving film, beautifully done, a tribute to all its stars but Gable was sorely taxed during the filming. The work on location was

Above: *As a second-rate song-and-dance man in* Idiot's Delight *(1939), Gable shuffled through 'Puttin' On The Ritz.'*

physically demanding and he didn't stint. Drugs and alcohol had left Marilyn barely able to say her lines some mornings and shooting rarely started on time. Still, Gable, the pro, was ready every day at nine and he left at five.

The Misfits was well received but Gable never knew it, for he died shortly after filming ended in 1960. It was the last movie for Monroe too. Gable's death left a hole in Hollywood no-one will ever fill. They just don't make stars like that any more. Hard to know, hard to get close to, but invariably courteous and genial, Clark Gable was a man who never let fame go to his head. When it comes to class, style, and masculine image, Gable still tops the list.

Clark Gable: *Forbidden Paradise* 24, *The Merry Widow* 25, *The Pacemakers* 25, *The Plastic Age* 25, *North Star* 25, *The Painted Desert* 31, *The Easiest Way* 31, *Dance Fools Dance* 31, *The Finger Points* 31, *The Secret Six* 31, *A Free Soul* 31, *Laughing Sinners* 31, *Night Nurse* 31, *Sporting Blood* 31, *Susan Lennox: Her Fall and Rise* 31, *Possessed* 31, *Hell's Divers* 31, *Polly of the Circus* 32, *Strange Interlude* 32, *Red Dust* 32, *No Man of her Own* 32, *The White Sister* 33, *Hold Your Man* 33, *Night Flight* 33, *Dancing Lady* 33, *It Happened One Night* 34, *Fugitive Lovers* 34, *Men in White* 34, *Manhattan Melodrama* 34, *Chained* 34, *Forsaking All Others* 34, *After Office Hours* 35. *Call of the Wild* 35, *China Seas* 35, *Mutiny on the Bounty* 35, *Wife Versus Secretary* 36, *San Francisco* 36, *Cain and Mabel* 36, *Love on the Run* 36, *Parnell* 37, *Saratoga* 37, *Test Pilot* 37, *Too Hot to Handle* 37, *Idiot's Delight* 39, *Gone With The Wind* 39, *Strange Cargo* 40, *Boom Town* 40, *Comrade X* 40, *They Met in Bombay* 41, *Honky Tonk* 41, *Somewhere I'll Find You* 42, *Adventure* 45, *The Hucksters* 47, *Homecoming* 48, *Command Decision* 48, *Any Number Can Play* 49, *Key to the City* 50, *To Please a Lady* 50, *Across the Wide Missouri* 51, *Lone Star* 52, *Never Let Me Go* 53, *Mogambo* 53, *Betrayed* 54, *Soldier of Fortune* 55, *The Tall Men* 55, *The King and Four Queens* 56, *Band of Angels* 57, *Run Silent Run Deep* 58, *Teacher's Pet* 58, *But Not For Me* 59, *It Started in Naples* 60, *The Misfits* 61.

Top: *One of Gable's earliest hits was* Red Dust *(1932) with Jean Harlow (right) and Mary Astor.*
Above: *Harlow and Gable were teamed for the last time in* Saratoga *(1937). Harlow died during filming and her scenes were completed with a stand-in.*
Below: *Clark Gable's Rhett Butler was always aware of every game Scarlett O'Hara tried to play. Widowed for the second time, she is soon to be swept away by his passionate wooing.*
Top right: *The surprise hit of 1934 was* It Happened One Night, *with Gable and Claudette Colbert. The hitchhiking scene is a classic.*
Right: *Gable's last film, released after his death, was* The Misfits *(1961), a stark melodrama which also starred Marilyn Monroe.*

Richard Gere

When *Newsweek* magazine did a cover story entitled 'The Male Idols, Hollywood's New Sex Symbols' – Richard Gere's picture appeared on the cover. Yet Gere has never been comfortable with the label sex symbol – he's an accomplished actor, one who has played a range of parts and has taken big chances.

What other sex symbol would interrupt a promising Hollywood career to go to Broadway and star in a depressing and uncommercial play about homosexuals in Nazi death camps? That's just what Gere did in 1980 when he returned to New York to star in the play *Bent*. As it turned out the show received marvelous notices and gave a boost to Gere's career. But to leave Hollywood to appear on stage – particularly in such a play – was extremely risky for a budding sex symbol.

'I certainly could have played characters that focus on sex and book myself up for the next 10 years for an enormous amount of money.' Gere told *Newsweek*. 'I've consciously not done that. I've chosen roles because they allow me to explore things that I haven't done before.' However, there is no denying the fact that Gere has appeared naked or nearly so in most of his films and that accounts for part of his popularity, so the sex symbol image is not entirely inappropriate.

Gere was born in 1949 in a middle-class suburb of Syracuse, New York. He dropped out of the University of Massachusetts after his second year and spent several years trying to 'make it' as a stage actor. He was not an immediate success, but unlike many young actors he was able to land parts regularly in regional theaters or off Broadway.

He was an understudy in the Broadway production of the musical *Grease*, and played Danny Zuko in the London production. He impressed the British theater world so much that he was able to do a season with the Young Vic – a rare opportunity for an American actor.

Gere's film career began with *Report to the Commissioner* (75) in which he played a pimp. In *Baby Blue Marine* (76), another rarely seen film, he was a shell-shocked marine whose hair had turned white. *Days of Heaven* (78) was a poetic and beautifully photographed film, but once again, a film that practically no one saw. Gere was good but the scenery was better.

Gere did make an impact in *Looking for Mr Goodbar* (77) where he played a stoned hustler who dances around Diane Keaton's bedroom swinging a knife and wearing only a jockstrap. The scene was electrifying but Gere was more menacing than appealing and the film itself was grim and not nearly as popular as the producers had expected.

There were a few minor roles, and then a big one as the high-priced male prostitute in *American Gigolo* (79). Once again Gere looked great with his expensive silk suits and fancy shirts, as he delivered a solid performance as a basically unsympathetic and empty character. It was after *Gigolo* that he decided to do *Bent* on Broadway.

Gere's 'breakthrough film' was an old fashioned sentimental romance, *An Officer and a Gentleman* (82). Gere played a tough but basically vulnerable punk who is turned into a naval officer and a gentleman by military discipline and the love of a good woman. The film was the 'sleeper' of 1982. It grossed millions, pulled in a flock of awards and solidified Gere's leading man status.

After *Officer*, Gere's next film effort was *Breathless* (83), a remake of the 1960 French 'New Wave' classic of the same name. Gere played Jess Lujack a dopey yet lovable

---

Left: *Richard Gere, seen here in* American Gigolo *(1979), is typical of the talent in the new Hollywood. An actor making his way without the power of a major studio behind him, Gere is equally at home in the theater.*

Above: *As the officer cadet in* An Officer and A Gentleman *(1982), Gere's performance was outstanding and believable as was that of his co-star Debra Winger, seen here at the dance where they meet.*

Middle right: *An early performance which brought Gere some notice and notoriety was that of one of Diane Keaton's pick-ups in the depressing film* Looking for Mr Goodbar *(1977) based on the novel by Judith Rossner.*

Right: Yanks *(1979) was the beautifully filmed story of the American troops in England during World War II. Gere's love interest in the film was Lisa Eilbacher, who played an innocent English girl.*

Top left: *With Michael Caine in* Beyond the Limit *(1983), a strange film based on Graham Greene's novel* The Honorary Consul. *Gere played Caine's best friend who falls in love with Caine's wife. The film was not a hit.*

Above: *As the petty thief in the 1983 remake of the* nouvelle vague *classic* Breathless, *Gere hoped to get away from sex symbol roles which seemed to be all he was offered. Although the remake was not as effective as the original (1961), Gere should have remembered that that film had been the start of Jean-Paul Belmondo's career as a sex symbol. Turning the plot around and setting the film in California did not make any difference. Audience reaction was blasé to everything except Gere's body.*

petty thief. The film did not please the critics or real film devotees who compared it unfavorably to the earlier version. It was called a ripoff of a classic and an exploitation film. Despite a generous, some contended too generous, display of the now-famous Gere body, the public didn't respond with much enthusiasm either. The average filmgoer found the picture confusing, boring and pointless.

His next film, *Beyond the Limit* (83), based on a Graham Greene novel and co-starring Michael Caine, fared even more poorly with the critics and the public. While *Breathless* was something of a *cause celebré*, *Limit* was practically ignored. People were beginning to wonder if there was anything more to Richard Gere than a great body.

Indeed there is. Gere is a serious, hard working actor. He has never been swept up in the Hollywood life. Though he can command big bucks for films he is willing to take far less than top dollar for a part he considers to be good. Now what he must do is pick a few more winners.

Richard Gere: *Report to the Commissioner 75, Baby Blue Marine 76, Looking for Mr Goodbar 77, Days of Heaven 78, Bloodbrothers 78, Yanks 79, American Gigolo 79, Officer and a Gentleman 82, Breathless 83, Beyond the Limit 83, Cotton Club 84*

Cary Grant

We admire him, we envy him. We never resent him. Gossip columnists may tell us the real Cary Grant is sad or troubled; we don't buy it. With his style, elegance and supreme self-confidence Cary Grant is the success story of our dreams, the one man the whole world wants fervently to believe has got it all.

He gets away with things on screen no one else would dare try. Embracing even the most beautiful movie star he manages to appear more embarrassed than aroused, yet every woman in the audience wishes she were the one he was nervously clutching. He can do a double-take equal to Edward Everett Horton without looking foolish. Pratfalls and slapstick never rob him of his debonair cool. He's got just the right amount of English accent. It gives him an extra dollop of class, but doesn't make him sound like a fop or a cad. Not the least bit haughty, in no way a snob, he moves gracefully through a milieu of glamor and luxury. What's more he seems to have defeated time. He's the only romantic lead to grow better looking with age. Yes, Cary Grant really is Mr Lucky.

He didn't start lucky. His real name is Archibald Alex Leach, which certainly doesn't sound promising. Archie was born into a poor family in Bristol, England on 18 January 1904. When he was 12 his mother had a 'nervous breakdown' and was placed in a nursing home. In his early teens Archie ran away to join a troupe of acrobats. One of his grandfathers had been an actor, so vaudeville and the theater weren't mere abstractions to him. As a member of the Pender Troupe he learned stilt walking, juggling, mime and clown routines. It was excellent training.

Left: *Cary Grant, the debonair star of more than 75 movies, including some of the great screwball comedies of the 1930s and Alfred Hitchcock adventure films, retired at the height of his career in 1966.*

In 1920 the troupe came to America and Archie remained after they left. Times were hard for the future Cary Grant. He was a lifeguard at Coney Island and a song-and-dance man doing mostly one night stands. He even carried advertising boards to earn the rent money. He played the vaudeville circuit whenever he could. At his lowest point he was an audience plant with a mind reading act.

In 1923 Archie returned to England where he got a few small parts in musical comedies. However, he returned to New York, hoping for a real break. Almira Sessions, a vaudeville star, helped the struggling young actor find work. Archie was grateful for her help and later, as Cary Grant, regularly offered her parts in his films. By the late 1920s Archie had made it to Broadway, playing the juvenile in the Oscar Hammerstein II show *Golden Dawn*. It ran for 184 performances.

Polly, with Fred Allen, and *Boom-Boom*, starring Jeanette MacDonald, followed. *Boom-Boom* lasted 72 performances. In the fall of 1929 Archie won the leading role in *Wonderful Night*, opposite Gladys Baxter. The stock market crash wiped out ticket sales and 1931 found Archie in St Louis doing a summer season of operettas. Then there was one more Broadway musical, *Nikki*, starring Fay Wray, but it bombed. Archie, prospects dim, was out of work again. He did, however, get something out of *Nikki*, the first half of what would one day be a very famous name. In *Nikki*, he'd played a character called Cary Lockwood. Archie liked 'Cary' lots better than 'Archie.'

Paramount was making films in New York and like every other studio, looking for actors with good voices, because most pictures were now made with sound. Cary had a brief appearance in a ten-minute one-reeler. The camera emphasized his devilish good looks and the highly photogenic Cary was told to go to Hollywood. Deciding

When Britain declared war on Germany after the German invasion of Poland, Cary Grant met with the British ambassador in Washington DC. Grant was encouraged to remain in Hollywood making films, using his wealth and influence to promote the Allied cause. *His Girl Friday* (40) was a comedy with Rosalind Russell. *My Favorite Wife* (40) starred Irene Dunne as a shipwrecked wife who returns home to cause a multitude of comic problems for husband Cary Grant. *The Philadelphia Story* (41), with Katharine Hepburn, is a classic.

Cary Grant was earning $150,000 per movie by then, a princely sum. Movie director and genius Alfred Hitchcock wanted and got him for *Suspicion* (41), based on the mystery novel *Before the Fact*. Hitchcock tried to follow the original plot, which would make Cary Grant the murderer. RKO studio bigwigs forced Hitchcock to change the ending, exonerating Grant but destroying the film. In a way the multi-talented Grant was trapped by his own success. Rarely was he allowed to play more than a light comic romantic lead. Though he excelled at such parts he was versatile enough to take on more challenging roles. Grant's good looks and bon vivant style would have made him believable as an unrepentant rogue or classy villain, but in Hollywood type casting was a way of life.

Penny Serenade (41), a rather weepy movie, won Cary Grant his first Oscar nomination. Ironically, he would never win a Best Actor Academy Award though he did receive a special Oscar in 1970 honoring him for his total acting career. He would acquire other honors. He made the top ten box office list three times during the 1940s and came in second in 1959. He stayed on the list for the next eight years. Grant also holds the record for movies shown at New York's Radio City Music Hall, which always had its pick of the crop; 28 films for a total playing time of 113 weeks. Runners-up are Katharine Hepburn and Fred Astaire.

In 1942 Cary Grant legalized his screen name in June and in July married heiress Barbara Hutton. Though he was busy making movies, one, *Mr Lucky* (43), stands out. Grant plays gambler Joe Adams, who escapes the draft by assuming the identity of a dead friend. It was a serious role and Grant played the cheating and chiseling Adams with great charm. Alas, though his wickedness is seductive, Joe Adams is redeemed by the film's end. *Destination Tokyo* (44) was a war movie, *Once Upon a Time* (44) a darling piece of fluff about a dancing caterpillar. *Arsenic and Old Lace* (44), based on the Broadway hit, was a masterpiece, with Grant doing some of his best mugging and miming.

None But The Lonely Heart (44), based on Richard Llewellyn's best seller, had Grant playing a Cockney tramp. The movie, directed and written by Clifford Odets, gained Grant his second Academy Award nomination. *Night and Day* (46) was based very loosely on the life of Cole Porter. Next followed a string of winners: *Notorious* (46), directed by Hitchcock, co-starring Ingrid Bergman; *The Bachelor and the Bobby Soxer* (47) with grown-up Shirley Temple, a real money maker; *The Bishop's Wife* (47); *Mr Blanding Builds His Dream House* (48); *Every Girl Should Be Married* (48) with Betsy Drake, and *I Was a Male War Bride* (49), with Cary as a Frenchman wishing to

marry WAC Ann Sheridan, The Oomph Girl.

Although by 1950 Cary Grant was making $200,000 a picture and would continue working steadily, his star status began to drop. Mistakes hurt him. He turned down a couple of biggies, *Sabrina* and the remake of *A Star is Born*. He almost got *The Third Man* but the deal fell through. Grant's career sprang to life again, thanks to Hitchcock's *To Catch a Thief* (55), a dazzler with Grace Kelly, set in Monaco. *An Affair to Remember* (57) with Deborah Kerr did well. So did *The Pride and the Passion* (57) with Sophia Loren and *Indiscreet* (58) with Ingrid Bergman. *North By Northwest* (59) was vintage Hitchcock and vintage Cary Grant.

Grant made a deal with Universal that netted him the biggest financial gain of his whole career. Eager to get him for *Operation Petticoat* (60), the slumping studio gave Grant 75 per cent of the picture's profits. He made a cool three million. Grant scored again at the box office with *That Touch of Mink* (62) with Doris Day. An apparently immortal Romeo, he was urbane and handsome in the delightful thriller, *Charade* (63) with Audrey Hepburn. *Father Goose* (64), was his last good film.

Over the years his name had been linked to many glamorous women. Sophia Loren claimed he was the only man in her life who offered any real competition to Carlo Ponti. In 1965 Grant married the young actress Dyan Cannon. She bore him his only child, daughter Jennifer, born in 1966, when Grant was over 60. The couple's 1968 divorce proceedings were raucous. She accused him of using LSD and beating her up in front of the servants. The public could care less. When Grant retired from films in 1966 he was, despite his age, at the height of his fame and fortune; his legend untarnished, his image agleam.

Cary Grant, blessed with looks, talent, wit, stardom

Left: *The three stars of* The Philadelphia Story *(1941): James Stewart, Grant and Kathrine Hepburn at the end of this famous screwball comedy.*

Right: *Grant first co-starred with Hepburn in* Bringing Up Baby *(1938). Baby was the leopard.*

Lower right: *In* Night and Day *(1946) Grant played composer-lyricist Cole Porter and Monty Woolley played himself. The woman between them is Jane Wyman.*

Bottom right: *Cary Grant confronts his homicidal aunts, Jean Adair and Josephine Hull, in* Arsenic and Old Lace *(1944). This famous black comedy was directed by Frank Capra.*

and longevity is the ideal man about town, even man of the world. He once said, 'I play myself to perfection.' Aren't we lucky he does.

Cary Grant: *Singapore Sue* 32, *This is the Night* 32, *Sinners in the Sun* 32, *Merrily We Go to Hell* 32, *The Devil and the Deep* 32, *Blonde Venus* 32, *Hot Saturday* 32, *Madame Butterfly* 32, *She Done Him Wrong* 33, *Woman Accused* 33, *The Eagle and the Hawk* 33, *Gambling Ship* 33, *I'm No Angel* 33, *Alice in Wonderland* 33, *Thirty Day Princess* 34, *Born to be Bad* 34, *Kiss and Make Up* 34, *Ladies Should Listen* 34, *Enter Madam* 35, *Wings in the Dark* 35, *The Last Outpost* 35, *Pirate Party on Catalina Island* 36, *Sylvia Scarlett* 36, *Big Brown Eyes* 36, *Suzy* 36, *Wedding Present* 36, *When You're in Love* 37, *Riches and Romance* 37, *Topper* 37, *Toast of New York* 37, *The Awful Truth* 37, *Bringing Up Baby* 38, *Holiday* 38, *Topper Takes a Trip* 39, *Gunga Din* 39, *Only Angels Have Wings* 39, *In Name Only* 39, *His Girl Friday* 40, *My Favorite Wife* 40, *The Howards of Virginia* 40, *The Philadelphia Story* 41, *Penny Serenade* 41, *Suspicion* 41, *The Talk of the Town* 42, *Once Upon a Honeymoon* 42, *Mr Lucky* 43, *Road to Victory* 44, *Destination Tokyo* 44, *Once Upon a Time* 44, *None But the Lonely Heart* 44, *Arsenic and Old Lace* 44, *Without Reservations* 46, *Night and Day* 46, *Notorious* 46, *The Bachelor and the Bobby Soxer* 47, *The Bishop's Wife* 47, *Mr Blandings Builds His Dream House* 48, *Every Girl Should Be Married* 48, *I Was a Male War Bride* 49, *Crisis* 50, *People Will Talk* 51, *Room For One More* 52, *Monkey Business* 52, *Dream Wife* 53, *To Catch a Thief* 55, *The Pride and the Passion* 57, *An Affair to Remember* 57, *Kiss Them For Me* 57, *Indiscreet* 58, *Houseboat* 58, *North By Northwest* 59, *Operation Petticoat* 60, *The Grass is Greener* 61, *That Touch of Mink* 62, *The Big Parade of Comedy* 63, *Charade* 63, *Father Goose* 64, *Walk, Don't Run* 66.

Paul Newman

The word that best describes Paul Newman is sane. Despite good looks, boyish charm, lots of talent, and the bluest eyes this side of Frank Sinatra, Paul Newman has kept a balanced perspective on life through decades of Hollywood stardom. In a world of bloated egos he is reasonably modest. In a milieu where marriages last maybe ten minutes his has endured since 1958. A devoted father, a concerned citizen who actively supports liberal causes, Newman is distinctly an anomaly for Tinseltown, going so far as choosing to live in Connecticut instead of LA. No hollow man, he's led a full life, with its share of sorrow as well as happiness. If all this makes Newman sound like a respectable but dull Mr Nice Guy then how do you explain his love affair with race-car driving, his infatuation with the excitement of speed? Though Paul Newman has never won an Academy Award he's achieved one success that makes him the envy of actors everywhere. In the early 1970s Paul Newman became for awhile the number-one box-office star in the world.

Newman was born into a wealthy family in Cleveland, Ohio in 1925. Newman was a good athlete but not a particularly good student and he spent part of his youth in a state of aimless drift, clear about only one thing: that he did not want to go into the family sporting goods business. During World War II he served in the Navy, but saw little action. Then he went to Kenyon College in Ohio, studying banking and economics and playing football so well he considered turning pro. There was no hint of his real future yet. Newman was definitely not an early bloomer.

On a fluke he tried out for the lead in a school play and got it. After that he was hooked, abandoning sports for drama. Summer stock in Wisconsin followed. Then he joined an acting company in Illinois where he met his first wife, Jackie Witte. Newman returned to the family business briefly when his father fell ill, and ran it successfully. Like it or not, he had a knack for business.

Paul Newman became a father himself in 1950. A year later, with his wife's encouragement, Newman enrolled in the Yale Drama School, expecting to become an English professor. He was 26 years old. But he was a good actor who loved performing and he decided to try to break into professional theater. He went to New York City where he picked up television roles quickly and was soon accepted by the prestigious Actor's Studio. A role in *Picnic* on Broadway in 1953 was all it took to win him a five-year contract with Warner Brothers. Newman went to Hollywood. But, determined to avoid a life style he detested, he left his family back east and got away from California whenever he could.

His distrust of Hollywood seemed justified when he was forced to appear in *The Silver Chalice* (54). This film, his first, was such an embarrassment to him that years later when it showed up on television he took out a newspaper ad bordered in black apologising for it. Newman, like James Dean, Marlon Brando and a number of other New York actors who represented a new breed of film stars, had to contend with an outmoded dictatorial studio system. Movie stars of the 30s and 40s were literally owned by the studios. The studio brass decided what roles actors played, the color of their hair, and even who they dated. Newman and his ilk were much too independent for such nonsense, and the studios, their imperial powers slipping, had to compromise. But it was a struggle.

Left: *As Detective Lew Harper, a role he has played in two films, Paul Newman typifies the modern hard-boiled West Coast private eye. His ordinary good looks and subtle style of acting make any performance believable.*

Left: *As the aspiring senator in* The Candidate *(1972), Redford alienated his wife and friends, but the audience loved him.*
Middle left: Jeremiah Johnson *(1972), the story of an early mountain man, was filmed on location in Utah.*
Bottom left: *Based on the political exposé by* Washington Post *reporters Bob Woodward and Carl Bernstein,* All the President's Men *(1976) was a believable thriller. Redford played Woodward and Hoffman Bernstein.*
Above: The Three Days of The Condor *(1975) was an entertaining thriller about a conspiracy in the CIA.*
Right: *With Mia Farrow as Daisy Buchanan in* The Great Gatsby *(1974), an overdone adaptation of an American classic.*
Far right: *Aerial stunts were the highlight of* The Great Waldo Pepper *(1975), a film about a World War I ace in the twenties.*
Below: *In* The Natural *(1984), Redford played a baseball player, who makes a miraculous comeback.*

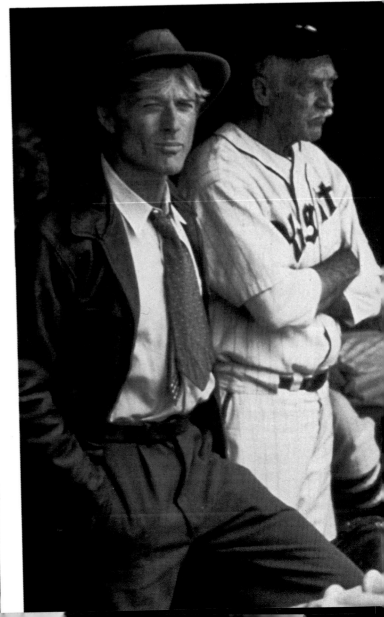

Johnson (72), a commercial success. Redford practically upstaged the charismatic Barbra Streisand in *The Way We Were* (73), a nostalgic love story and one of the best romantic movies to be made in years. *The Sting* (73), a charming piece of fluff set to a ragtime beat, paired Redford with Newman once more. It was a blockbuster. Redford hit the top ten box office moneymakers list and got a Best Actor Oscar nomination as well.

Though *The Great Gatsby* (74) with Mia Farrow was hyped plenty, it was not a commercial success. *The Great Waldo Pepper* (75) allowed Redford to show off his athletic prowess. Playing a 1920s daredevil pilot he did some of the stunts himself. Redford got a cool million and a half for *The Three Days of the Condor* (75), a first-rate spy thriller.

Redford produced and appeared in *All The President's Men* (76), based on Bob Woodward and Carl Bernstein's book about the Watergate investigation. Redford was Woodward and Dustin Hoffman was Bernstein. A compelling and historically significant movie, it stands as one of Redford's finest achievements.

Redford is distinctly not a workaholic when it comes to movies and except for a supporting role in *A Bridge Too Far* (77), he wasn't on screen again till *The Electric Horseman* (79), with Jane Fonda, and *Brubaker* (79). Perhaps he was busy with his new career, directing pictures. He won the Academy Award for the Best Director for *Ordinary People* (80).

Five years were to pass between *Brubaker* and Redford's next film *The Natural* (84), based on the novel by Bernard Malamud. A beautifully done rather mysterious movie, it is a fairy tale story of a baseball player. A big success, the movie proves that Redford can stay away from the screen or return at will. The Sundance Kid is Hollywood's Sun King and audiences can't get enough of him.

Robert Redford: *War Hunt* 62, *Situation Hopeless but not Serious* 65, *Inside Daisy Clover* 66, *The Chase* 66, *This Property is Condemned* 66, *Barefoot in the Park* 67, *Butch Cassidy and the Sundance Kid* 69, *Downhill Racer* 69, *Tell Them Willie Boy is Here* 70, *Little Fauss and Big Halsy* 70, *The Hot Rock* 72, *The Candidate* 72, *Jeremiah Johnson* 72, *The Way We Were* 73, *The Sting* 73, *The Great Gatsby* 74, *The Great Waldo Pepper* 75, *The Three Days of the Condor* 75, *All The President's Men* 76, *A Bridge Too Far* 77, *The Electric Horseman* 79, *Brubaker* 79, *The Natural* 84.

Burt Reynolds

Burt Reynolds is good-looking, has a good sense of humor, and has made a good bit of money playing good old boys. Unfortunately, like most sex symbols, he has trouble persuading people to take him seriously as an actor. Since his brave appearance as the first male nude centerfold in the April 1972 issue of *Cosmopolitan*, critics have tended to dismiss Reynolds as just another chunk of pulchritude. But Burt Reynolds, whose charm is reminiscent of Cary Grant's, is really far more than just another, shall we say, pretty face.

Reynolds was born in Georgia in 1936, but was raised primarily in Florida where his father was the police chief of a town called Riviera Beach. Reynolds's grandmother on his father's side was a Cherokee Indian and Reynolds would play a lot of Indian roles later in his career. As a kid he was wild, nothing excessive, mostly drinking and brawling. Because of his superb athletic ability, luck came his way in the form of a football scholarship to Florida State University. He was about to turn pro when he was injured in a car crash. A teacher spotted his acting talent and Reynolds found himself in the drama department. In 1955 he quit school and came to New York. Summer stock and a stint at City Center led him to television, and it was television, not movies, that would make him a success.

He was an Indian blacksmith in TV's long running *Gunsmoke* and he played the lead in short-lived TV series called *Hawk*. In the early 1960s Reynolds began appearing in films, chiefly as a stunt man. In 1963 he married British actress Judy Carne, best known as the 'sock-it-to-me' girl on television's popular *Laugh-In* show. They were divorced in 1966. In the early 1970s Reynolds's name was linked to singer and television star Dinah Shore and he started appearing on television talk shows regularly. He showed a ready wit and his playful way of poking fun at himself made him a popular guest with Merv Griffin and Johnny Carson. Once Reynolds became a familiar face on television he landed a good film role, appearing with Jon Voight in *Deliverance* (72), a film about a backwoods river trip which becomes a ghastly nightmare. The movie was a hit and Reynolds became a movie star.

He lampooned his hunk image in Woody Allen's *Everything You Always Wanted to Know About Sex But Were Afraid to Ask* (72). He wasn't on screen long but he was memorably funny. He turned down James Bond, reluctant to follow in Sean Connery's footsteps, but made up for it with *The Longest Yard* (74), about a prison football game. An exciting movie, it grossed a bundle.

Smokey and the Bandit (77), a car-chase picture, cost a mere four million but it literally took the public by storm and wound up one of the highest grossing films of the decade, up there with *Star Wars* and *Rocky*. Actress Sally Field starred in the movie with Reynolds and for several years they were a twosome in the gossip columns. That year Reynolds made it to number four on the top ten box office list and shared a *Time* magazine cover with Clint Eastwood.

Semi-Tough (77), a satire of pro football, wasn't a blockbuster but it did well. By now Reynolds was desperately eager to be thought of as something more than a beer-drinking jock or screen lover-boy and he did his best to get good scripts. It wasn't easy. The good scripts went to Paul Newman. Reynolds was pigeonholed as strictly a commercial success. *Hooper* (78) was another smash.

Left: *A remarkable actor with a great sense of timing, Burt Reynolds is best known for a series of slapstick 'good ol' boy' movies, but his first major success was the nightmarish adventure film* Deliverance.

Above: *As businessmen lost in the Georgia wilderness, Reynolds starred with Jon Voight in* Deliverance *(1972).*
Right: *A more typical role is that of the bootlegger in* Smokey and the Bandit *(1977). Seen here with Pat McCormick (right) and Paul Williams, Reynolds delights in hiring stars to play cameo roles.*
Top right: *Co-starring Rachel Ward,* Sharkey's Machine *(1981) was a mystery about a detective who falls for a gangster's girlfriend.*

Left: *Reynolds starred with Sally Fields and Dom de Luise in* The End *(1978), a black comedy about a man with a terminal illness who tries to cheat death by committing suicide.*
Top right: *With Dom de Luise in* Cannonball Run *(1981), a comedy about an illegal transcontinental road race.*
Bottom right: *Goldie Hawn played Reynolds' partner and new wife in the comedy* Best Friends *(1982).*

Reynolds's best chance to break out of typecasting came with *The End* (78), and it was no mean achievement being funny in a film about death, but his film career didn't alter course. *Starting Over* (79) won Oscar nominations for his co-stars Jill Clayburgh and Candice Bergen, but not for him. He starred in and directed *Sharkey's Machine* (81). *Best Friends* (82) showed Reynolds at his most delightful, moving from a meaningful relationship to a messy marriage with Goldie Hawn. In his spare time Reynolds invested heavily in real estate and restaurants, especially in the South. He also performed at the Burt Reynolds Dinner Theater in his hometown and gave large sums of money to the theater and athletic departments at his alma mater.

Burt Reynolds remains a witty appealing personality on screen, an actor whose scope and range have yet to be realized. Too bad Alfred Hitchcock isn't around to take advantage of Reynolds's agility, charm and presence. Still, there's every chance Burt Reynolds will get the recogni-

tion he craves. After all, Hollywood forgave Marilyn Monroe for posing naked. Doesn't Burt Reynolds deserve as much?

Burt Reynolds: *Angel Baby* 61, *Armored Command* 61, *Operation CIA* 65, *Navajo Joe* 66, *Fade-In* 68, *Impasse* 69, *Shark* 69, *100 Rifles* 69, *Sam Whiskey* 69, *Skullduggery* 70, *Deliverance* 72, *Fuzz* 72, *Everything You Always Wanted to Know About Sex but Were Afraid to Ask* 72, *The Shamus* 73, *White Lightning* 73, *The Man Who Loved Cat Dancing* 73, *The Longest Yard* 74, *W W and The Dixie Dancekings* 74, *At Long Last Love* 74, *Hustle* 75, *Lucky Lady* 75, *Gator* 76, *Silent Movie* 76, *Nickelodeon* 76, *Smokey and the Bandit* 77, *Semi-Tough* 77, *The End* 78, *Hooper* 78, *Starting Over* 79, *Smokey and the Bandit II* 80, *Rough Cut* 80, *The Cannonball Run* 81, *Paternity* 81, *Sharkey's Machine* 81, *Best Friends* 82, *The Best Little Whorehouse in Texas* 82, *Stroker Ace* 83, *The Man Who Loved Women* 83, *Cannonball Run II* 84.

Tom Selleck

Alone among the stars in this book Tom Selleck is a creation of television. He made some films early in his career but they were not notably successful. He achieved his fame on a TV series, but his attempts to turn TV popularity into big screen stardom have not succeeded – 'yet.' One critic said Selleck was a 'master of television behaviour in much the same way Clark Gable…was a master of movie behaviour.'

Selleck was born in Detroit, Michigan on 29 January 1945. When he was about five his father, an investment executive, moved the family to Sherman Oaks, California, near Los Angeles. It was a tightly knit, conservative family and Selleck recalls that on their twenty-first birthday each of the children got a gold watch from their father for not smoking, drinking or swearing.

In high school Selleck was a standout athlete and won an athletic scholarship to the University of Southern California. He was majoring in business administration when a school drama coach told him that he was good looking enough to try out for some television commercials. He also appeared on the game show *The Dating Game* – but he didn't get the girl.

There is some irony in his career, for while Selleck often proclaims his own conservative values and fights hard against any attempt to pin a 'swinger' label on him, he got his first film assignment on the recommendation of Mae West. The film was *Myra Breckinridge* (70), a tasteless adaptation of Gore Vidal's tasteless novel about a gay man who has a sex change operation and becomes a 'sex goddess.' Selleck played the role of a 'stud.'

His second film was *Seven Minutes* (71) directed by Russ Meyer, a master of the cheap and vulgar sex film. In both these films Selleck was lucky because his role was so small as to almost escape notice.

After that start his film career had nowhere to go but up, and it did, though not very far. His next film and first major role was in *Daughters of Satan* (72), a low-budget horror film. There were a few more bit parts, but while his film career did not prosper his TV career did.

Selleck appeared in a number of made for TV movies and he spent a year and a half in the soap opera *The Young and The Restless*. He also had a recurring role in the popular detective series *The Rockford Files*. But the bulk of his income came from commercials.

Selleck was under contract to Universal Television, and the company was looking around for the right vehicle for him. He made a number of pilots but nothing seemed to work out. Then he was given the script for *Magnum*, a proposed show about a private detective in Hawaii. Selleck liked the idea well enough but thought that the hero was a little too perfect. He wanted to play a character who, 'would not always get the girl, and he would occasionally blunder badly. . .' The script was revised along the lines Selleck had suggested, and by 1980 it was ready to go into production.

Then came one of those critical moments that sometime occur in the career of an actor. Tom Selleck was approached by Stephen Spielberg and asked to play the lead in a new picture that he was doing with George Lucas. The picture had the strange title of *Raiders of the Lost Ark*. Selleck wanted the part but he couldn't get out of his TV obligation. As it turned out, there was a strike that delayed the start of the *Magnum* series, but by that time the role of Indiana Jones had been given to Harrison Ford.

Would Selleck's career have been different if he had been able to star in *Raiders*? There is no way of knowing. But

---

Left: *TV star turned movie star, Tom Selleck starred in a spoof of thirties adventure movies,* High Road To China *(1983). Not a great success, the film did lead to other parts. Selleck is best known for a popular television series and a number of well-regarded made-for-television movies. Perhaps it is this phenomenon more than any other that makes him a star of the eighties.*

Left: *Selleck began his career in Hollywood as part of May West's entourage and appeared with her in the forgettable* Myra Breckinridge *(1970). A series of small parts followed, including that of a corpse in* Coma *(1978).*

Above: Lassiter, *which was released in 1984, was another tribute to the movies of an earlier era. The romantic tale of a cat-burglar in the thirties, the film co-starred ex-model Lauren Hutton.*

Magnum PI catapulted Tom Selleck to the top of TV popularity.

The show opened to generally good reviews. The critics particularly liked Selleck's sense of humor and his character's 'endearing flaws.' By the second season *Magnum* was one of TV's top rated shows and Selleck himself was consistently voted the most popular male star on a regular series.

The schedule for shooting a regular one-hour TV series is exhausting, and Selleck himself has the reputation of being an exceptionally hard worker with little time for off-screen high living. During his breaks from shooting *Magnum* he makes movies.

Divorce Wars: A Love Story (81) was a made for TV film about an ambitious divorce lawyer who finds himself being sued for divorce. The film was well received. However, when he tried to take his new found celebrity to the big screen he stumbled badly. *High Road to China* (83) was an inept but expensive adventure flick. When it opened people lined up to see it, but negative reviews and word of mouth soon killed business. His second major film *Lassiter* (84) did better at the box office, but it was no blockbuster – Selleck remains a TV star, but he plans future films.

Selleck guards his privacy fiercely and estimates that he is spending $10,000 a week on legal fees mainly to pursue suits against gossip columns and scandal sheets. A cautious and practical man, he fears overexposure. He knows the *Magnum* series will not last forever and he doesn't want the public to be tired of him by the time he starts looking for another job.

Selleck was married in 1970 to model Jacquelyn Ray. The couple were divorced in 1982, but Selleck maintains a close relationship with his ex-wife and her teen-aged son from a former marriage.

In the days when the film studios had total control of a star's life and of the information that was fed to the press, the public only knew what the press office wanted it to know. That sort of control of information no longer exists. Tom Selleck has worked hard at maintaining a nice guy image – fortunately for him, that's not difficult, because everyone who has worked with him says he really is a nice guy.

What's his appeal? *Magnum* co-star John Hillerman says, 'Women look at Tom Selleck and say "My God, I want to go to bed with him." Men look at him and say, "I'd like to spend an evening having a drink with that guy." His appeal is universal.'

Whether this appeal will persist beyond *Magnum* only time will tell.

Tom Selleck: *Myra Breckinridge* 70, *Seven Minutes* 71, *Daughters of Satan* 72, *Midway* 76, *Coma* 78, *Divorce Wars* 82, *Shadow Riders* 82, *High Road To China* 83, *Lassiter* 84.

Sylvester Stallone

Perhaps no actor has ever been more thoroughly identified with the character he plays than Sylvester Stallone has been with Rocky Balboa. Stallone may actually be trapped in the character for the public has been reluctant to accept him in any other role.

But it is a trap entirely of his own making. Unlike actors of an earlier era, Stallone was not typecast by a heartless studio. Rocky Balboa is Sylvester Stallone's creation. And it's a solid gold trap, for the character catapulted its creator from down-at-the-heels obscurity to being one of the most popular and richest actors in the world. It is a case where truth really is stranger than fiction. Stallone's triumph has been more astonishing than Rocky's.

Sylvester Stallone was born in 1946 in the section of New York known, for good reasons, as Hell's Kitchen. His parents, Sicilian immigrants, moved to Silver Spring, Maryland when he was five. After his parents' divorce, the boy lived primarily in a rundown section of Philadelphia, which was to serve as the background for *Rocky*. Much of the time he was in and out of foster homes and in and out of school. A difficult pupil, Stallone was reportedly kicked out of 14 different schools in 11 years. He did manage to attend college briefly and then spent some time roaming around Europe.

His well-muscled physique got him either an athletic scholarship at the American School in Switzerland, or a job as a bouncer. Accounts differ. It was in Europe that Stallone picked up his desire to become an actor and when he returned to America he was enrolled briefly in the drama department at the University of Miami where in-structors advised him against pursuing an acting career. He refused to be discouraged.

For a while the closest he was able to get to the theater was a job as an usher in New York's Baronet movie theater. He appeared in a never-released sexploitation film *Kitty and Studs* – Stallone was Studs. He had a part in the nude off-Broadway drama *Score*, and he played a minotaur in a play, *Desire Caught by the Tail* written by Pablo Picasso and presented in Brooklyn. It was his physique, not his acting talent that got him his jobs.

His first role in a film that was released was an uncredited bit part as a hood in Woody Allen's *Bananas* (71).

Stallone then got a break of sorts. This was a pretty good part in a low budget New York-made film, *The Lords of Flatbush* (74), a nostalgic look at Brooklyn gangs of the 1950s. He gave a winning performance as a dumb, brawny but rather likable punk. Stallone also did some of the writing for the film, and got an 'additional dialogue' credit. His performance attracted favorable notices. The film could have been a big boost for his career, but it wasn't. There were no further leads offered so Stallone went to Hollywood to look for additional film work.

His next role was a bit part in the film version of Neil Simon's *The Prisoner of Second Avenue* (75). In the film he portrays an innocent bystander who is pursued and assaulted by an enraged Jack Lemmon. Can you imagine Jack Lemmon beating up on Rocky?

There were a few more small roles, usually as a muscular hoodlum, but his career was going nowhere. Nearly broke, and with his wife pregnant, Stallone decided to make his own breaks by writing a starring vehicle for himself. He wrote the first draft of *Rocky* in three days. It was a deliberately old-fashioned, optimistic, sentimental type of film about a down-and-out boxer from Phi-

Left: *In F.I.S.T. (1978), his first movie after the award-winning* Rocky, *Sylvester Stallone tried to break away from that character to play a trucker who rises through the ranks to lead the union and is corrupted in the process.*

Left: *Part of the success of* Rocky *(1976) was due to the charm of the love story. Talia Shire was nominated for an Academy Award for her performance as Rocky's girl.*
Above: *By* Rocky III *(1982) the conflict had resolved itself as Rocky and Stallone fought to stay at the top.*
Below: *In* Rhinestone *(1984) Stallone, as a cab driver turned singer, teamed up with country-and-western superstar Dolly Parton.*

Top: Paradise Alley *(1978), the tale of three brothers growing up in the slums of New York, was based on a novel by Stallone.*
Below: *Stallone's latest stint at directing has been* Staying Alive *(1983), a sequel to* Saturday Night Fever, *starring John Travolta.*

ladelphia who, through grit and determination, becomes a winner.

United Artists was interested in the film, but Stallone didn't want to just sell a script, he wanted the starring role. He finally sold the script for a relatively small sum on the condition that he play the lead and get a ten percent share of the profits, if any. It was a big gamble, and it paid off more handsomely than even Stallone might have dreamed. *Rocky* was the sleeper of 1974. Not only did it gross millions, it was also nominated for a flock of Academy Awards. It won best picture and *Rocky's* director John Avildsen won best director. *Rocky* even took an Oscar for best editing. Stallone had been nominated as best actor and his script as best screenplay, but he won neither of those. His disappointment was clearly evident to the millions who watched the award show on TV, and it was the first public display of what has now become the notorious Stallone arrogance.

Still, even without a personal Oscar, Sylvester Stallone's triumph had been spectacular, and he was quickly signed to a five picture contract by UA, given a big budget and lots of freedom to make the kind of pictures he wanted. His next effort was *F.I.S.T.* (78) which he also helped to write. The title stood for Federation of International State Truckers and Stallone played the Jimmy Hoffa-type character who rises to the top of the union and becomes corrupted by his power and gangster associates. *F.I.S.T.* was an ambitious, curious and interesting film – Stallone was detestable yet lovable – and he couldn't carry it off, perhaps no one could. After the stunning triumph of *Rocky, F.I.S.T.* was a real disappointment. His next effort, *Paradise Alley* (78), was about a gang of street kids trying to use wrestling as a way up. Stallone wrote, directed and starred in this one, and it was an even bigger flop. People were beginning to ask whether Stallone's short career was over.

So Sylvester Stallone returned to the tried and true, and made *Rocky II*. This time he starred, wrote and directed. Had the public forgotten Rocky Balboa? It had not. Though most critics, including many who had liked the original, found *Rocky II* (79) laughable, it was a smash. So was *Rocky III* (82). Are there further adventures of Rocky Balboa in Sylvester Stallone's future? Only time will tell. In the meantime his directing and writing career has prospered. He wrote and directed *Staying Alive* (83) starring John Travolta, another Italian-American screen hero.

Travolta's career had been slipping since his unexpected triumph in *Saturday Night Fever* (77). Stallone decided to trace the further career of the Brooklyn disco dancer, now turned Broadway chorus boy. Once again the critics snickered, but the public, particularly the teen-aged public, made the film a major success.

Sylvester Stallone has the golden touch – sometime.

Sylvester Stallone: *Bananas* 71, *The Lords of Flatbush* 74, *The Prisoner of Second Avenue* 75, *Capone* 75, *Death Race 2000* 75, *Farewell My Lovely* 75, *Cannonball* 76, *Rocky* 76, *No Place to Hide* 77, *F.I.S.T.* 78, *Paradise Alley* 78, *Rocky II* 79, *Nighthawks* 81, *Victory* 81, *Rocky III* 82, *First Blood* 82, *Staying Alive* 83, *Rhinestone* 84.

Rudolph Valentino

H e was born Rodolfo Alfonzo Raffaele Pierre Phi-libert Guglielmi de Valentina d'Antonguolla on 6 May 1895 in Castellaneta, Italy. He would dispense with most of the names and become Rudolph Valentino, the legendary idol of the silent screen. The son of an army veterinarian, Valentino was sent to a military academy at the age of 13. He tried the Navy, he tried studying agriculture. He failed at both. He did, however, show a remarkable talent for spending money, and at age 17 having squandered a good portion of the family wealth, tried his luck in Paris, but wound up begging on street corners. In 1913 he set out for New York.

In Brooklyn, Valentino boarded with Italian immigrant families and worked as a landscape gardener, dishwasher and waiter. A graceful young man with smouldering dark eyes he soon found his true vocation as a taxi dancer. Stories about Valentino's unsavory past abound, some true, some no doubt exaggerated. There is no question, however, that he was picked up by the New York City police a number of times and booked on suspicion of petty theft and blackmail.

Valentino moved out of the ten-cents-a dance class and into the big time when he replaced Clifton Webb as the partner of popular dancer Bonnie Glass. He changed partners again, (stability was not Valentino's strong suit) but his success as a dancer did not prevent his spending several days in New York's gloomy detention prison, The Tombs. He left New York hastily after that, a member of the cast of a musical called *The Masked Model*. It closed in Ogden, Utah, leaving the cast stranded. This posed no

problem for the ever resourceful and adaptable Valentino and once more he landed on his shapely feet. After a brief stint dancing in San Francisco, Valentino reached the fabled city of Hollywood, America's Babylon.

A friendly person by nature, Rudolph Valentino quickly made a lot of new acquaintances, both male and female, and they helped him get bit parts in films. Generally he played a seductive dancer or an oily villain, usually with a moustache. There was *Alimony* (18) and *The Blackmailer* (18). He had a leading role in *A Society Sensation* (18), was in *All Night* (18) and for a change played the nice guy in *The Delicious Little Devil* (19) with Mae Murray. An apache dancer in Vitagraph's *A Rogue's Romance* (19), he had a starring role in *Virtuous Sinners* (19), played an Irishman in *The Big Little Person* (19), had a lead in *The Eyes of Youth* (19) and was a villain in a Dorothy Gish comedy, *Out of Luck* (19). *The Cheater* (20), *Passion's Playground* (20) and *Once to Every Woman* (20) kept Valentino working.

In 1920 he married actress Jean Acker who supposedly locked him out of the bridal suite on their wedding night so that the marriage was never consummated. Not consummating marriages doesn't sound like Valentino's style but whatever the truth of the story this wedding would come back to haunt him. He was arrested later on a bigamy charge, having never bothered to make sure that his first marriage was really dissolved before embarking upon a second.

Screenwriter June Mathis was a power at Metro and she took a liking to Valentino, to the point of demanding that this basically unknown young man be given the lead in *The Four Horsemen of the Apocalypse* (21). Thanks to her he got the role of the South American ne'er-do-well who becomes a hero in France during World War I. Valentino's golden moment had arrived.

Left: *Costumed for his most famous part, Rudolph Valentino was symbolic of the love of the exotic that flooded America after World War I. Such novels as* The Sheik *were naturals for movie treatment as the motion picture industry began to expand.*

Left: *Despite its age and some unintentional humor* The Four Horsemen of the Apocalypse *(1921), Valentino's first major movie, is a very powerful piece of cinema. The famous tango scene is still remarkably sexy, and gives the modern moviegoer an idea of what made the women of the twenties crazy about Valentino.*

Bottom left: *Even in rags at the beginning of* Blood and Sand *(1922), Valentino has remarkable stage presence. In later scenes, as the triumphant matador complete with brillantined hair and the traditional suit of lights, he was electrifying.*

Below and right: *With Vilma Banky in* The Son of the Sheik *(1926). Even then early Hollywood had learned that a sequel could be just as successful as an original film. Women could not get enough of Valentino in a burnoose, and the promise of a night under the desert stars with such a sheik.*

Above: *One of Wayne's best roles during World War II was as General Claire Chennault in* Flying Tigers *(1942), the story of American fliers battling the Japanese in the skies over China.*

John Wayne: *Mother Machree* 28, *Hangman's House* 28, *Salute* 29, *Words and Music* 29, *Men Without Women* 30, *Rough Romance* 30, *Cheer Up and Smile* 30, *The Big Trail* 30, *Girls Demand Excitement* 31, *Three Girls Lost* 31, *Men Are Like That* 31, *Maker of Men* 31, *Range Feud* 31, *Shadow of the Eagle* 32, *The Hurricane Express* 32, *Haunted Gold* 32, *Texas Cyclone* 32, *Lady and Gent* 32, *Two Fisted Law* 32, *Ride Him Cowboy* 32, *The Big Stampede* 32, *The Telegraph Trail* 33, *His Private Secretary* 33, *Central Airport* 33, *Somewhere in Sonora* 33, *The Life of Jimmy Dolan* 33, *Baby Face* 33, *The Man from Monterey* 33, *Sagebrush Trail* 33, *Riders of Destiny* 33, *The Three Mesquiteers* 33, *West of the Divide* 34, *The Lucky Texan* 34, *Blue Steel* 34, *The Man from Utah* 34, *Randy Rides Alone* 34, *The Star Packer* 34, *The Trail Beyond* 34, *'Neath Arizona Skies* 34, *Texas Terror* 34, *Rainbow Valley* 35, *Paradise Canyon* 35, *The Dawn Rider* 35, *The Desert Trail* 35, *Westward Ho* 35, *The New Frontier* 35, *The Lawless Range* 35, *The Lawless Nineties* 36, *The King of the Pecos* 36, *The Oregon Trail* 36, *Winds of the Wasteland* 36, *The Sea Spoilers* 36, *The Lonely Trail* 36, *Conflict* 36, *California Straight Ahead* 37, *I Cover the War* 37, *Idol of the Crowds* 37, *Adventure's End* 37, *Born to the West* 37, *Pals of the Saddle* 38, *Overland Stage Riders* 38, *Santa Fe Stampede* 38, *Red River Range* 38, *Stagecoach* 39, *The Night Riders* 39, *Three Texas Steers* 39, *Wyoming Outlaw* 39, *New Frontier* 39, *Allegheny Uprising* 39, *The Dark Command* 40, *Three Faces West* 40, *The Long Voyage Home* 40, *Seven Sinners* 40, *A Man Betrayed* 41, *Lady from Louisiana* 41, *The Shepherd of the Hills* 41, *Lady for a Night* 42, *Reap the Wild Wind* 42, *The Spoilers* 42, *In Old California* 42, *Flying Tigers* 42, *Reunion in France* 42, *Pittsburgh* 42, *A Lady Takes a Chance* 43, *War of the Wildcats* 43, *The Fighting Seabees* 44, *Tall in the Saddle* 44, *Flame of the Barbary Coast* 45, *Back to Bataan* 45, *Dakota* 45, *They Were Expendable* 45, *Without Reservations* 46, *Angel and the Badman* 47, *Tycoon* 47, *Fort Apache* 48, *Red River* 48, *Three Godfathers* 49, *Wake of the Red Witch* 49, *She Wore a Yellow Ribbon* 49, *The Fighting Kentuckian* 49, *Sands of Iwo Jima* 49, *Rio Grande* 50, *Operation Pacific* 51, *Flying Leathernecks* 51, *The Quiet Man* 52, *Big Jim McLain* 52, *Trouble Along The Way* 53, *Island in the Sky* 53, *Hondo* 53, *The High and the Mighty* 54, *The Sea Chase* 55, *Blood Alley* 55, *The Conqueror* 56, *The Searchers* 56, *The Wings of Eagles* 57, *Jet Pilot* 57, *Legend of the Lost* 57, *I Married a Woman* 58, *The Barbarian and the Geisha* 58, *Rio Bravo* 59, *The Horse Soldiers* 59, *The Alamo* 60, *North to Alaska* 60, *The Comancheros* 61, *The Man Who Shot Liberty Valance* 62, *Hatari!* 62, *The Longest Day* 63, *How the West Was Won* 62, *Donovan's Reef* 63, *McLintock!* 63, *Circus World* 64, *The Greatest Story Ever Told* 65, *In Harm's Way* 65, *The Sons of Katie Elder* 65, *Cast a Giant Shadow* 66, *The War Wagon* 67, *El Dorado* 67, *The Green Berets* 68, *Hellfighters* 69, *True Grit* 69, *The Undefeated* 69, *Chisum* 70, *Rio Lobo* 70, *Big Jake* 71, *The Cowboys* 72, *The Train Robbers* 73, *Cahill US Marshal* 73, *McQ* 74, *Brannigan* 75, *Rooster Cogburn* 75, *The Shootist* 76.

Left: *John Wayne, as most people remember him, the cowboy hero of many westerns. His career began with many B-pictures, but flourished through such classic parts as the Ringo Kid in* Stagecoach, *Davy Crockett in* The Alamo, *Rooster Cogburn in* True Grit, *and the dying gunfighter in* The Shootist.

Index

Credits

Phototheque: 2 (Gable), 12, 16, 26 top, 54 right, 61 top, 63 bottom right, 70 bottom right, 72, 73 middle, 82 top left and right, 82-83 bottom, 83 top left and right, 86 bottom right, 87 both, 94 bottom, 98-99 bottom, 102 bottom left, 108 all.
All other pictures: Bison Picture Library
Special thanks to Jerry Ohlingers movie stills store for their help with this book.